SHARON O'CONNOR'S
MENUS AND MUSIC VOLUME III

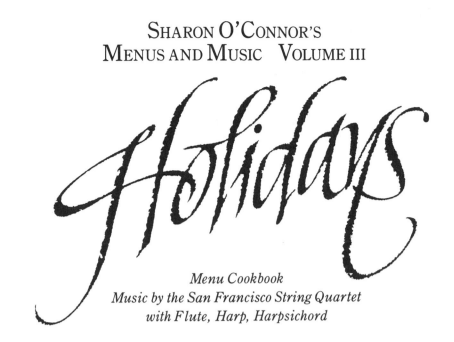

Holidays

Menu Cookbook
Music by the San Francisco String Quartet
with Flute, Harp, Harpsichord

Menus and Music Productions, Inc.
Piedmont, California

Photo of menu on page 10 from the book Classic Menu Design: From The
Collection Of The New York Public Library, by Reynaldo Alejandro used by
permission of PBC International, Inc.

The Tortilla Soup recipe on page 169 from The Mansion on Turtle Creek
Cookbook by Dean Fearing, published by Weidenfeld and Nicholson, New
York City.

Library of Congress Cataloging-in-Publication Data
O'Connor, Sharon
Menus and Music™
Holidays
Menu Cookbook
Music by the San Francisco String Quartet
with Flute, Harp, Harpsichord

Includes Index
1. Cookery 2. Entertaining
I. Title
89-092217
ISBN 0-9615150-2-3 (pbk.)

Menus and Music is published by

Menus and Music Productions, Inc.
1462 66th Street
Emeryville, CA 94608
(510) 658-9100

Book and Cover Design by Jacqueline Jones Design
Cover Photograph by Michael LaMotte
Food Styling by Amy Nathan
Typography by Ann Flanagan Typography

Manufactured in the United States of America
10 9

Contents

ACKNOWLEDGMENTS

I would like to thank the many people who made this volume possible.

To Nathan Rubin, James Shallenberger, and Duncan Johnstone, fellow members of the San Francisco String Quartet. For the beautiful flute playing, Alan Cox; harp, Dan Levitan; harpsichord, Giddeon Meir. To Martha Rubin of Fog City Sound for music production and moral support. Thanks for the generous help and support of Ray Dolby, Ioan Allen, and Tom Bruchs from Dolby Laboratories Inc.

My gratitude to all the chefs, restaurants, hotels, inns, and resorts who generously contributed menus and recipes to the cookbook.

To my editor, Carolyn Miller, once again thanks for being so thorough and flexible. Thanks to Lori Merish for more than a year of hard work.

To Jacqueline Jones and Suzie Skugstad for their wonderful design and support of this project.

To my friend Jeremy Cohen, whose violin is pictured on the cover, and my friend Angela Koregelos, whose flute is pictured on the cover. To Georgia Deaver for the beautiful calligraphy. To Reynaldo Alejandro of the New York Public Library.

I want to thank most of all John Coreris for his unending support and encouragement, and Claire and Caitlin for constantly reminding me that love and joy is what the holidays are all about.

*This book is dedicated
to the memory of David George.*

INTRODUCTION

During the holiday season we take time to feed our souls with beautiful music and our bodies with fine food. As we gather each year the sounds, smells, and tastes of these holidays bring memories of happy familiarity. I hope this volume will add to the merriment as the wonderful smell of your feast fills the house and the sound of music invites your guests to rejoice and join you in celebrating the season.

The two loves of my life are great music and great food—and I think they are inseparable. As the cellist and leader of the San Francisco String Quartet I have observed firsthand how people love the combination of beautiful music and fine food. I founded the San Francisco String Quartet in 1975, and we began performing dinner music in the Sheraton-Palace Hotel's Garden Court, which has been called "the most beautiful dining room in the world." Our dinner concerts consist of quartets by composers from Bach to Debussy, intermingled with shorter works. We nurture a love of chamber music while people nourish themselves.

Our standards remain the same whether we are playing background dinner music or a concert in a hall. In fact, classical music was not always meant to be performed only in concert halls—composers wrote for opera houses, and also for dining rooms, parlors, and gardens. Mozart wrote his serenades, cassations, divertimenti, and notturni for these places, and Telemann, inventing an even more specific genre, wrote his "Table Music." Before 1800, composers showed no disinclination to serve prosaic needs (or to hear their works accompanied by the sounds of conversations, or of knives and forks). Nor did they let such needs limit their craft—the music has survived for more than two centuries.

After performing for twelve years in the Garden Court, this grand room now feels like my living room. I decided to ask chefs from similarly historic and grand rooms from all over America to contribute holiday menus and recipes for this volume of *Menus and Music*. Most of these rooms have the elegance and romance of a historical setting, and all are places I would like to take my family for a festive holiday dinner! In planning this book and tape, I made sure the collection of recipes would be complemented by the music on the accompanying cassette by giving each chef a list of the pieces that were to be recorded. I asked them to create a meal that would be enriched by this music.

This collection of recipes features the holiday specialities of the contributing restaurants, hotels, or resorts, and it also reflects regional American specialties. There is a wonderful diversity in the menus and in the ingredients. The chefs have patiently and generously explained their recipes to me during the past year. Their menus and recipes are traditional, but the chefs all have a firm contemporary insistence on the use of fresh ingredients at the peak of their flavor. I have enjoyed tremendously visiting in person or being an armchair traveler to twenty-one of the most wonderful dining rooms in America!

The music recorded here is festive but not specific to any one holiday, so that it may be enjoyed from Thanksgiving through January or for that matter all year round. The program includes some of my favorites from the chamber music repertoire and can be enjoyed during your kitchen preparations, while you are dining, or as an after-dinner concert. It can be a festive part of a holiday celebration with family and friends, and it can help provide a moment of quiet reflection during a hectic time. Music can create and sustain the mood you want for your party, infuse a dinner party with energy, and bring people together like nothing else.

I hope this volume of *Menus and Music* will help you create the right ambience for a wonderful holiday feast and make your celebration the merrier. Rejoice in the season!

—Sharon O'Connor

MUSICAL MENUS

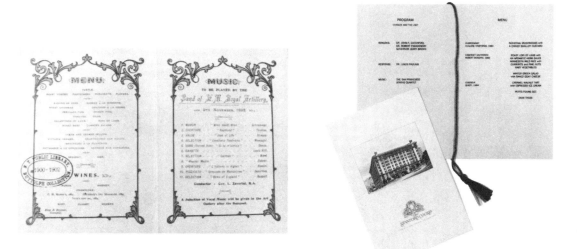

Menus have been historically associated with music, as can be seen from the above menu of 1893, reproduced from the culinary collection of the New York Public Library. Also shown is a menu from a dinner at the Stanford Court Hotel in San Francisco in 1988 for which the San Francisco String Quartet provided the music.

Toulouse-Lautrec considered cookery an art and practiced this art himself. He also designed his own menus and thereby combined the arts of cookery and painting. The photographs of Ansel Adams were used to illustrate the menus of the Ahwahnee Hotel while he was the director of the hotel's famous Christmas Bracebridge Dinners.®

You could make your own menus to give as keepsakes of your celebrations. Hand lettering and painting are wonderful alternatives to professional printing. A Thanksgiving menu might list the menu on one side and the lyrics to the song "America" on the other. You could include a list of people who will be making toasts during the dinner or some anecdotes that apply to the occasion. The back page might be used for autographs of people who attended the party. Have fun!

Notes About The Composers

Arcangelo Corelli (1653–1713)
Concerto Grosso Op. 6 No. 8
Fatto per la notte di Natale

Corelli was an Italian violin virtuoso and composer of a modest number of very influential pieces. His greatest achievement was the creation of the concerto grosso form; he is also regarded as the founder of modern violin technique. He was the first composer to derive his fame exclusively from instrumental composition and also the first to produce "classic" instrumental works that were admired and studied long after their idiom became outmoded. Corelli's orchestration was based solely on strings plus the instruments for the figured bass. The size of his orchestra varied from having each part played by a single instrument to several on each part depending on the size of the room and the formality of the occasion. He once conducted an orchestra of 150 strings for a coronation. The concerto grosso *Fatto per la notte di Natale* was published near the end of Corelli's life.

Marcel Grandjany (1891–1975)
Aria in Classic Style

Grandjany was a brilliant French harpist who became an American citizen in 1945. He was known for his faultless technique and the beauty of his tone. His influence as a harp teacher at the Juilliard School of Music was immense, and his many solo and ensemble harp compositions are extremely well written for the instrument.

George Frederick Handel (1685–1759)
Pifa from the Messiah

Handel, a naturalized English composer of German birth, was one of the greatest composers of the Baroque age in both vocal and instrumental music. All of his major works were composed within an astonishingly short time; the three weeks he spent on the *Messiah* is the most famous of many examples. The *Messiah* is his only sacred oratorio and expresses the deepest aspirations of the Anglican religious spirit. At the time Handel completed the *Messiah*, the middle class was strongly suspicious of the hedonistic element in art, however, and regarded the theater as a haunt of sin and moral laxity. When Handel gave the first London performance of the *Messiah* he advertised it without a title as a "New and Sacred Oratorio" to avoid giving offence. This tactic failed, and even before the performance there was an attempt in the press to damn the enterprise as blasphemous because an oratorio was "an Act of Religion" unsuited to the playhouse. The work was not a success at first; it didn't impress London audiences until Handel began to perform it for charity in the Foundling Hospital Chapel. The Pifa recorded here is a short instrumental insertion and serves as a link in a chain of pictures making up the Christmas scene. The inspiration for this movement is said to derive from the Christmas music of Calabrian shepherds, which Handel probably heard in Italy in his youth. The title "Pifa" (from *Pifferari*) suggests this. The shepherds in the field are represented by traditional pastoral symbols that include pedal points and a siciliano rhythm. The angels proclaim their Christmas message over the earth and fade away in the gradually subsiding conclusion.

Wolfgang Amadeus Mozart (1756–1791)
Flute Quartet in D Major K. 285

Mozart is regarded as the most universal composer in the history of Western music. He excelled in every musical medium current in his time, especially in chamber music for strings, piano concertos, and opera. The Flute Quartet in D major was a commission from a wealthy Dutch flutist and was composed in Mannheim in 1777. It is essentially a string quartet, with the leading part played by the flute instead of the first violin. In the first movement the strings play an accompaniment part for the flute rather than taking part in a dialogue on equal terms. The extremely beautiful thirty-five-bar Adagio is not a developed slow movement but rather an introduction to the Finale. The concluding Rondo is true chamber music, and we are indebted to Mozart forever for, in William Blake's phrase, "catching joy as it flies."

Henry Purcell (1659–1695)
Abdelazer Suite
Rondeau, Air, Minuet, Air

Purcell was one of the greatest composers of the Baroque period and also one of the greatest of all English composers. He is known for his chamber works, church music, and music for the stage. Purcell received a commission to provide an overture and eight act-tunes for a revival of Aphra Behn's play Abdelazer, which was presented at the Drury Lane Theatre. The music he composed for this play didn't attain the popularity it deserved until well into the twentieth century, when Benjamin Britten used the Rondeau from *Abdelazer* in his set of variations *A Young Person's Guide to the Orchestra*.

Ralph Vaughan Williams (1872–1958)
"Fantasia on Greensleeves"

Vaughan Williams was the most important English composer of his generation as well as being a teacher, writer, and conductor. He was especially interested in English folksong and developed a thoroughly English yet distinctly personal style. "My Lady Greensleeves" was a folk song popular during the reign of Queen Elizabeth, and Shakespeare referred to it as one of the most popular tunes of his day. Sir John Stainer arranged it into the Christmas carol "What Child Is This," and it was entered as the "The Old Year Now Away Is Fled" in the *Oxford Book of Carols* in 1928. Vaughan Williams used the tune "Greensleeves" in his opera *Sir John in Love*, and Ralph Greaves arranged from the score of this opera the Fantasia for strings and harp with one or two optional flutes. The folk tune "Lovely Joan" is the basis of the middle section. It was first performed in 1934, with Vaughan Williams conducting.

Antonio Vivaldi (1678–1741)
"Winter" from *The Four Seasons*, Op. 8 No. 4

Vivaldi was the father of the modern concerto and a great violin virtuoso. He
made the instrument a star performer by his own innovative virtuosity and by
modifying the concerto grosso form to allow the violin (and other instruments
as well) to function as a solo voice singing out over the orchestra. Vivaldi wrote
as many as five hundred concertos for various instruments. He was also a
pioneer of orchestral programme music such as his four concertos portraying
the seasons, which he composed in 1725. Printed with *The Four Seasons* was a
quartet of sonnets, one for each concerto. The poet is unknown, but the sonnets
easily could have been written by Vivaldi himself as a guide to the pictorial con-
tent of the music.

WINTER

To shiver, tingling with the chilling snows . . .
To run with stamping feet, while every moment
A fierce wind blows
And teeth are all a-chatter with the cold . . .
To sit in quiet by a happy fireside
While those abroad are pelted by the rain . . .
To walk upon the sleet with timorous tread
for fear of fall, at each turn taking care
Against the slippery way . . .
To romp upon the ice, to leap and run
Until the frozen surface cracks and breaks,
The while blow from Eternity's iron gate,
Sirroco, Boreas and the fighting winds . . .
This is the winter, and it giveth joy.

Aaron Copland 1900-
"Simple Gifts"
Shaker song arranged by Aaron Copland

Aaron Copland is a distinguished American composer as well as a lecturer, writer, pianist, conductor, teacher, and, in his own words, "a good citizen of the Republic of Music." He is a winner of the Pullitzer Prize and an Oscar. His works based on American folk motives are especially popular. He used the Shaker tune "Simple Gifts" in his ballet *Appalachian Spring* as well as making a simple arrangement of the tune which he included in his "Old American Songs." After Copland made "Simple Gifts" famous it was adopted into the repertoire of schools, churches, and folk singers. The tune was transcribed for the San Francisco String quartet by James Shallenberger.

John Jacob Niles (1892–1980)
"I Wonder As I Wander"
Appalachian carol adapted and arranged by
John Jacob Niles

Niles was an American folk singer and authority on folk music. He made a special study of the music of the southern Appalachians. "I Wonder as I Wander" was one of the Appalachian tunes he collected, adapted, and arranged for voice and piano. He also made arrangements of about a thousand other folk songs and wrote choral works in folk style. "I Wonder As I Wander" was transcribed for the San Francisco String Quartet by James Shallenberger.

THE AHWAHNEE

The grand Ahwahnee Hotel is set on the valley floor of Yosemite National Park. Glacier-carved Yosemite became a national park in 1890 and is famous worldwide for its unexcelled natural beauty. When white men drove the Awahneechee Indians out of the valley, they named the valley Yosemite, a corruption of the Indian word *ohamite* meaning "grizzly bear."

The Ahwahnee Hotel opened in 1927, and its design was masterful. Its massive six-story structure is faced with granite and concrete beams stained to look like redwood. Throughout the hotel's public rooms are placed a priceless collection of paintings, photographs, and Indian baskets and rugs. The Ahawahnee is a National Historic Landmark.

In summer guests enjoy seeing Yosemite's geologic marvels, biking, river rafting, rock climbing, and High Sierra hiking. In winter, there is cross-country and downhill skiing, iceskating, and the Yosemite Vintners' and Chefs' Holidays.

The Ahwahnee dining room is often described as the most beautiful restaurant in America. It has a twenty-four-foot-tall trestle-beamed ceiling, massive floor-to-ceiling windows framing views of forests and meadows, and wrought-iron chandeliers. Fine cuisine is important at the Ahwahnee year round, but at no other time is it more important than on Christmas Day, when seven courses are synchronized with music and drama for the famous Bracebridge Dinner.® Ansel Adams, whose passion for photography and music were almost equal, was the Bracebridge Dinner® director for forty-two years, and his photographs illustrated the menus of the hotel. The following dinner menu from the Ahwahnee was presented to *Menus and Music* by Robert Anderson.

THE AHWAHNEE
MENU

Serves Twelve

Oyster Stew with Cheddar Toasts

Warm Cucumber Salad with Mixed Greens

Red Snapper with Pecans

Ragout of Duck and Escargots on Rösti Potatoes

Roast Tenderloin of Beef

Apple Cobbler with Sauce Anglaise

Oyster Stew

24 large oysters in their shells

3 tablespoons butter

6 tablespoons flour

1 tablespoon chopped shallots

1 cup Fish Stock, page 231

8 ounces mushrooms, diced

1 cup heavy cream

2 tablespoons chopped fresh dill

1 teaspoon salt

1 teaspoon ground white pepper

½ teaspoon cayenne

Juice from ½ lemon

In a large saucepan of boiling water, poach the oysters for 3 to 4 minutes. Remove the oysters from the boiling water with a slotted spoon. Drain and cool. Open the shells and remove the oysters, then chop them in half and set aside.

In another saucepan, melt the butter. Stir in the flour and cook over medium heat, stirring, for 3 minutes. Add the shallots and whisk in the fish stock. Bring the mixture to a boil, then reduce to a simmer. Add the mushrooms and cook for 3 to 4 minutes, then whisk in the cream. Add the seasonings. Add the oysters, heat for 2 or 3 minutes, and serve.

Makes 12 servings

Cheddar Toasts

8 ounces Cheddar cheese, finely grated

¼ cup minced fresh spinach leaves

1 teaspoon brown prepared mustard

1 tablespoon heavy cream

1 egg yolk

1 teaspoon Worcestershire sauce

½ teaspoon salt

½ teaspoon ground white pepper

12 slices sourdough bread

2 tablespoons butter, softened

Preheat the oven to 375°. In a medium-sized bowl, combine the cheese and spinach and set aside. In a large bowl, whisk together the mustard, cream, egg yolk, Worcestershire sauce, salt, and pepper. Add the cheese and spinach to the egg mixture, and stir until thoroughly blended.

Place the sourdough slices on a baking sheet. Lightly butter the sourdough slices on top and spoon equal amounts of the cheese mixture on each slice of bread. Bake in the preheated oven for 5 minutes, or until golden brown, and serve warm with oyster stew.

Makes 12 toasts

Warm Cucumber Salad
with Mixed Greens

6 cucumbers, peeled, seeded, and sliced

2 onions, sliced thin

1 garlic clove

¼ cup chopped fresh parsley

Salt and cracked pepper to taste

½ cup cider vinegar

⅓ cup sugar

½ cup vegetable oil

1 teaspoon Worcestershire sauce

Mixed greens, such as romaine, butter lettuce, dandelions, beet tops

In a saucepan, combine all the ingredients except for the mixed greens and warm over low heat. Place the mixed greens on a serving plate and pour the warm sauce over them. Mix quickly and serve at once.

Makes 12 servings

Red Snapper with Pecans

Twelve 6- to 7-ounce red snapper fillets

Salt and pepper to taste

Flour for dredging

2 to 3 tablespoons unsalted butter

2 to 3 tablespoons vegetable oil

1 cup (2 sticks) unsalted butter, at room temperature

1½ cups pecans

Juice of 2 lemons

Season the fillets with salt and pepper and dredge them in flour. In a sauté pan or skillet, heat the butter and oil and sauté the fish a few fillets at a time until golden brown, about 3 minutes on each side per batch, adding more butter and oil as needed. Remove the fillets from the pan as they brown; set aside and keep warm.

Discard the liquid in the pan and wipe it clean, then add the 1 cup butter. Melt the butter over low heat and continue to cook it until it is slightly browned, then add the pecans and cook another minute, taking care not to burn the butter. Quickly stir in the lemon juice. Remove the sauce from the heat and pour over the snapper. Serve immediately.

Makes 12 servings

Ragout of Duck and Escargots
on Rösti Potatoes

Three 3½-pound ducks

⅓ cup Grand Marnier

48 canned escargots

Sauce Velouté, following

6 medium red potatoes

Oil for frying

Juice and grated zest from 2 oranges

Preheat the oven to 450°. Fill a pot with salted water and rinse the ducks in the saline solution. Drain, dry with paper towels, and remove any excess fat from the ducks. Prick the skin of the ducks all over with a fork. Place the ducks on racks, reduce the oven heat to 350°, and roast for 1¼ to 1½ hours, or until a meat thermometer registers 180°. Let cool.

Remove the duck meat from the bones, reserving the bones for the orange sauce. Dice the meat and set aside. Remove all but 1 tablespoon of the duck fat from the roasting pan. Pour in the Grand Marnier; cook and stir over medium heat to deglaze the browned juices. Pour this mixture into a heavy saucepan, add the escargots and the velouté sauce, and simmer over low heat for 4 to 5 minutes.

Peel and grate the potatoes; mold into 12 balls. Pour oil to a depth of ¼ inch in a sauté pan or skillet; heat the oil and add half of the potatoes. Flatten the balls with a slotted spatula and cook them until brown on both sides; set aside and keep warm. Repeat with the remaining potato balls, adding more oil if necessary.

Whisk the orange juice into the ragout, then add the roast duck meat. Heat to warm through. Divide the potatoes among 12 serving plates, spoon the ragout over, and sprinkle with orange zest.

Makes 12 servings

Sauce Velouté

¼ cup vegetable oil

Reserved duck bones from Ragout of Duck, preceding

2 celery stalks, chopped

½ onion, chopped

1 carrot, peeled and chopped

1 teaspoon sugar

6 cups (1½ quarts) cold water

3 tablespoons butter

2 tablespoons flour

Salt and pepper to taste

In a heavy saucepan, heat the oil, then add the duck bones, celery, onion, and carrot and cook over medium heat to brown. Add the sugar and cook over medium heat for 3 to 5 minutes. Add the cold water and simmer for 4 hours. Strain through a sieve and discard the bones.

In another heavy saucepan, melt the butter over low heat. Stir in the flour and cook, stirring, for 2 or 3 minutes, then whisk in the strained liquid. Cook over medium heat, stirring occasionally, until thickened; season with salt and pepper.

Roast Tenderloin of Beef

1 tablespoon or more vegetable oil

One 6- to 7-pound beef tenderloin

Salt and pepper to taste

½ cup Jack Daniels whiskey

1 tablespoon brown sugar

Tabasco sauce to taste

12 carrots, peeled

1 bunch celery

24 medium new red potatoes

2 garlic bulbs, cleaned and separated into cloves

Preheat the oven to 400°. In a large sauté pan or skillet, heat the oil almost to smoking and quickly brown the tenderloin on all sides. Remove from the pan, season with salt and pepper, and set aside. Pour the Jack Daniels into the sauté pan or skillet, and cook over high heat to reduce the liquid; add the brown sugar and Tabasco. Reduce further to a thick syrup. Place the tenderloin in the pan and turn to glaze all over.

Cut the carrots and celery into ¼-inch-thick sticks about 2 inches long. Place the tenderloin in a baking pan along with the carrots, celery, potatoes, and garlic, and roast in the preheated oven for 25 to 30 minutes, or until the thickest part of the roast reaches an internal temperature of 120°. Allow to rest at room temperature for 20 minutes, then slice and serve with the roasted new potatoes and vegetables.

Makes 12 servings

Apple Cobbler with Sauce Anglaise

BATTER

6 eggs

2¾ cups sugar

1½ tablespoons baking powder

2¼ cups half and half

1 tablespoon vanilla extract

3 cups unbleached all-purpose flour

1½ pounds apples, peeled, cored, and cut into thin slices (about 4 cups sliced)

¼ cup apple brandy

¼ cup plus 2 teaspoons sugar

Sauce Anglaise, following

Preheat the oven to 325°. In a large bowl, beat the eggs, then stir in the 2¾ cups sugar and the baking powder. Whisk in the half and half and vanilla. With a wooden spoon, gradually stir in the flour, ½ cup at a time, and beat until smooth; set aside.

In a large bowl, toss the apples with the apple brandy and ¼ cup sugar. Butter the bottom of a 9-by-13-inch baking pan and sprinkle it with the remaining 2 teaspoons of the sugar. Spread the apple slices evenly in the pan and pour the batter over. Bake in the preheated oven for 45 minutes, or until golden brown. Serve warm, with sauce anglaise poured over.

Makes 12 servings

Sauce Anglaise

1 cup sugar

8 egg yolks

2 cups heavy cream, heated

In a large bowl, beat the sugar into the egg yolks until the mixture is thickened and pale yellow; gradually beat in the hot cream. Pour the mixture into the top of a double boiler over medium heat, and cook and stir constantly until it thickens; do not allow the sauce to come to a simmer. Strain the sauce through a fine sieve and let cool.

THE BREAKERS
Palm Beach, Florida

The Breakers is described in the National Register of Historic Places as "culturally significant in its reflection of twentieth-century grandeur" and is a designated National Landmark. The character of the hotel comes from its sixteenth-century Renaissance Italian architecture, the flamboyance of the Roaring Twenties when the hotel was built, and the subtropical ambience of Palm Beach. Leonard Schultze, architect of the Waldorf-Astoria in New York, was asked to rebuild the twice-burned Breakers in 1926. His design for the ocean-front hotel borrows from some of the most famous Italian Renaissance villas.

Recreational facilities at the 140-acre resort include golf, tennis, swimming, croquet, tennis, snorkeling in the hotel's namesake coral reef, workouts at the fitness center, and planned programs for children. The resort's luxurious grounds include a private strand of Palm Beach and groves of pine and palm trees sheltering flocks of exotic parrots.

The Breakers has five restaurants that serve a variety of fare ranging from a breakfast buffet and light snacks by the pool to elegant dinners and dancing in the fabulous Florentine Dining Room. The grand tradition of fine dining in the Florentine Room, paired with dancing to the music of a big band playing classic swing, remembers a more gracious era and a way of life that should never be forgotten.

For the ninth consecutive year the Breakers has received the Five-Diamond Award from the American Automobile Association (AAA). The hotel has received *Wine Spectator* magazine's Grand Award and has been rated as having one of the best wine lists in the world.

THE BREAKERS
MENU

Serves Six

Breakers' Mushroom Soup

Wild Rice and Mushrooms

Poached Apple Pears with Butternut Squash Purée

Trout au Bleu

Sautéed Cucumbers with Dill

Key Lime Pie

Breakers' Mushroom Soup

1 pound fresh mushrooms

6 tablespoons butter

1 cup chopped onions

½ cup chopped celery

3 garlic cloves, minced

5 tablespoons flour

9 cups chicken stock

2 cups heavy cream

4 tablespoons dry Marsala

4 tablespoons dry sherry

Salt and pepper to taste

Dash of nutmeg

Chop three fourths of the mushrooms and slice the remaining mushrooms. In a 4-quart saucepan, melt the butter. Add the chopped mushrooms, onion, celery, and garlic, and sauté until the mushrooms are tender. Dust the vegetables with the flour and cook and stir for about 2 minutes. Stirring constantly, add the chicken stock and bring to a boil; then reduce the heat and simmer for 8 to 10 minutes.

In a blender or a food processor, purée the soup in batches until smooth, then return it to the saucepan. Stir in the cream and cook over low heat for 5 minutes, stirring while the soup thickens. To serve, heat the Marsala and sherry in a small saucepan, then add the sliced mushrooms and cook a few minutes until tender. Add the wine mixture to the soup, adjust the seasoning, and serve.

Makes 8 to 10 servings

Wild Rice and Mushrooms

2 cups wild rice

6 cups water

1 teaspoon salt

2 tablespoons butter

12 small whole cultivated mushrooms

1 tablespoon chopped shallots

¼ cup dry white wine

¼ cup Veal stock, page 233, or beef broth

To prepare the rice, rinse thoroughly in cold water and drain. In a large, heavy saucepan, bring the water to a boil; add the salt and stir in the rice. Return to a boil, reduce heat to a simmer, cover, and cook slowly for 30 to 45 minutes, until the rice is fluffy and the water is absorbed. Set aside.

In a sauté pan or skillet, melt the butter over medium heat; sauté the mushrooms and shallots until the shallots are translucent. Add the white wine and veal stock. Bring to a boil and cook until the mixture is half the original volume; add the wild rice and mix well.

Makes 8 servings

Poached Apple Pears with Butternut Squash Purée

8 apple pears

5 cups water

4 cups sugar

2 butternut squashes

2 teaspoons salt

½ teaspoon ground pepper

1 teaspoon ground cinnamon

1 teaspoon ground nutmeg

2 tablespoons butter

Cut the top off each apple pear. Core and seed the apple pears but do not cut through the bottoms. Combine 4 cups of the water and the sugar in a saucepan and bring to a boil. Add the apple pears and simmer until they are tender, about 10 minutes. Remove from heat with a slotted spoon.

Peel the squash, then halve and remove the seeds. Cut the squash into 1-inch chunks. Put the squash into a saucepan, and add the remaining 1 cup of water. Cover the pan and bring to a boil. Reduce the heat and simmer over low heat until the squash are fork-tender, about 15 to 20 minutes. Drain off and discard the liquid. Mash the squash and season with salt and pepper, cinnamon, nutmeg, and butter. Pipe the squash into the center of the apple pears.

Makes 8 servings

Trout au Bleu

COURT BOUILLON

4 cups (1 quart) water

½ cup dry white wine

¼ cup distilled white vinegar

1 celery stalk

½ onion

1 medium carrot, peeled

2 whole cloves

2 bay leaves

½ teaspoon salt

½ teaspoon peppercorns

8 fresh whole trout (4 to 6 ounces each)

½ cup (1 stick) butter, melted

Parsley sprigs for garnish

In a stockpot, place the bouillon ingredients and bring to a boil over high heat. Place a skewer through the gills and tail of each trout so that each fish is curved into a half-circle. Poach in the boiling bouillon for 3 minutes, adding water as necessary so that the trout are completely immersed (you may want to do this in batches).

Garnish each trout with 1 tablespoon melted butter and a parsley sprig. Serve with boiled potatoes and sautéed cucumbers with dill, following.

Makes 8 servings

Sautéed Cucumbers with Dill

4 tablespoons butter

4 cucumbers, peeled, seeded, and sliced

3 tablespoons chopped fresh dill

In a sauté pan or skillet, melt the butter and sauté the cucumbers and dill for 30 seconds.

Makes 8 servings

Key Lime Pie

1 recipe Pie Pastry, page 232

3 egg yolks

⅔ cup fresh lime juice

3 cups sweetened condensed milk

TOPPING

1 cup heavy cream

2 or 3 tablespoons powdered sugar

1 or 2 limes, cut into paper-thin slices

Preheat the oven to 425°. Prepare the pastry dough, roll it out to a thin circle, and fit it into a 9 inch pie pan. Trim and crimp the edges and prick the insides with a fork. Fill with dried beans or pie weights and bake in the preheated oven for 10 minutes, or until set. Remove and set aside.

Reduce the oven to 350°. In a large bowl, blend together the egg yolks, lime juice, and condensed milk until smooth and creamy. Pour the mixture into the pie shell and bake for 15 minutes. Remove and cool in the refrigerator for at least 2 hours.

To make the topping, whip the cream, slowly adding the powdered sugar. Spread over the pie and decorate with slices of fresh lime. Serve at room temperature, but refrigerate if not serving within 3 hours of baking.

Makes one 9-inch pie

The Brown Palace Hotel

Denver's Brown Palace Hotel has a colorful and illustrious history. It is a National Historic Landmark because of the majesty of its architecture and is renowned because of the people who have graced its halls. Henry C. Brown opened the hotel in 1892 for the gold barons, and since then it has been a home to royalty as well as to international leaders and celebrities. The Brown Palace's unique triangular configuration enabled its architects to provide windows in each of the hotel's luxurious rooms and suites. It has impressive onyx-paneled walls and an atrium that soars past elaborately designed steel railings. Dominating the entire setting is the stained-glass ceiling that proclaims the hotel's Victorian heritage. Rocky Mountain spring water, revered for its purity and flavor, bubbles from the Brown's 750-foot-deep artesian well to faucets in every room.

Guests enjoy four seasons of recreational pleasures including skiing, trout fishing, and golf in the picturesque Rockies, as well as the cultural activities and sites of Denver.

Culinary delights at the Brown Palace include the award-winning cuisine of the Palace Arms, noted for its authentic Napoleonic setting. The Brown Palace's chef, Gary Levine, created the following menu for *Menus and Music*.

THE BROWN PALACE HOTEL
MENU

Serves Twelve

*Smoked Trout Terrine with
Cranberry-Horseradish Sauce*

Smithfield Ham with Red-Eye Hollandaise

Sweet Potato Soufflé

Roasted Turkey Roulades Stuffed with Dried Fruits

Orange-braised Mustard Greens

Saxon Plum Pudding with Armagnac Coulis

Granola Yogurt Parfait with Minted Rhubarb Compote

Smoked Trout Terrine with Cranberry-Horseradish Sauce

6 Rocky Mountain trout, skinned and boned

2 cups heavy cream

3 egg whites

Salt and pepper to taste

¼ cup chopped fresh cilantro

Cranberry-Horseradish Sauce, following

Light a wood or charcoal fire in a smoker or a covered grill. When the coals are covered evenly with gray ash, soak 1 cup apple wood chips in water to cover for 15 minutes. Sprinkle the soaked wood chips over the coals. Preheat the oven to 250°.

Place the trout in the smoker or on the grill, cover, and smoke the trout for 2½ minutes. Let cool and chop coarsely. Place the smoked trout in a blender or a food processer and purée, in batches if necessary. Pour into a bowl and beat in the cream and egg whites and purée until smooth. Add the salt, pepper, and cilantro.

Pour the trout mixture into buttered custard cups and place the molds in a baking pan. Pour water into the baking pan to halfway up the sides of the cups. Bake in the preheated oven for 35 to 45 minutes, or until a knife inserted in the center comes out clean. Remove the cups from the pan and let cool. Run a knife around the inside of each terrine and invert to unmold on a serving plate. Serve with cranberry-horseradish sauce.

Makes 12 servings

CRANBERRY-HORSERADISH SAUCE

½ cup chopped dried cranberries*

¼ cup vodka

1 cup heavy cream

½ cup finely grated fresh horseradish

Salt and pepper to taste

In a medium bowl, place the dried cranberries. Pour the vodka over them and soak for 15 minutes; drain.

In a deep bowl, beat the cream until thick. Stir in the horseradish, blending thoroughly. Season to taste and stir in the chopped cranberries.

*Available in some gourmet markets.

Smithfield Ham with Red-Eye Hollandaise

One 2-pound chunk Smithfield ham

2 bay leaves

1 onion

1 cup honey

2 cups strong black coffee

HOLLANDAISE SAUCE

4 egg yolks

4 teaspoons water

3½ cups (5 sticks) unsalted butter, melted

1 teaspoon Worcestershire sauce

½ teaspoon cayenne

Juice of 1 lemon

Reserved ½ cup reduced coffee and ham stock

3 tablespoons salt

½ cup red wine vinegar

24 quail eggs

12 scones or 6 English muffins

Butter for spreading

Soak the ham in water to cover for 2 days to remove the salt. In a large pot, boil the ham in fresh water to cover with the bay leaves and onion for 1¾ hours. Preheat the oven to 350°. Remove the ham from the pot, reserving the stock, and dry with paper towels. Brush the ham with honey, place in a baking pan, and bake in the preheated oven for 50 minutes.

Remove the ham from the baking pan. Pour the coffee and 1 cup of the ham stock into the baking pan; cook and stir over medium heat to deglaze the pan. Pour the liquid into a saucepan and boil to reduce it to about ½ cup; set aside.

To make the hollandaise, place the egg yolks in the top of a double boiler. Whisk them with the water and continue whisking until the egg mixture thickens. Remove from the heat and slowly whisk in the butter, pouring it in a very thin stream to make a thick sauce. Whisk in the Worcestershire sauce, cayenne, lemon juice, and the reduced ham stock and coffee mixture. Keep warm over very low heat.

In a large sauté pan or skillet, bring 2 inches of water to a simmer. Add the salt and red wine vinegar. Carefully break the quail eggs into a large shallow bowl. Slide the eggs into the simmering liquid and cook for 2 minutes; remove with a slotted spoon and let cool. To serve, cut the ham into thin slices; lightly toast and butter the scones or English muffin halves. Top each scone or muffin half with a few slices of ham and 2 quail eggs, then pour the hollandaise sauce over.

Makes 12 servings

Sweet Potato Soufflé

2 pounds sweet potatoes

½ cup (1 stick) butter, melted

5 tablespoons cornstarch

1 teaspoon ground allspice

1 teaspoon ground cumin

Salt and pepper to taste

5 eggs, separated

Preheat the oven to 400°. Bake the sweet potatoes for 45 minutes, or until they are tender throughout when tested with a knife. Remove the sweet potatoes from the oven, leaving the oven at 400°. Scoop the flesh from the skins and place in a large bowl. Mash the sweet potatoes with a large spoon. Combine the butter with the cornstarch and add this mixture to the sweet potatoes; blend until smooth. Add the allspice, cumin, salt, and pepper; then beat in the egg yolks. In a large bowl, beat the egg whites until stiff but not dry. Fold them into the sweet potato mixture.

Butter two 4-cup soufflé dishes and divide the sweet potato mixture between them; then bake in the 400° oven for 35 minutes or until puffed and firm.

Makes 12 servings

Roasted Turkey Roulades Stuffed
with Dried Fruits

3 cups mixed dried apricots, prunes, and dates, coarsely chopped

Twelve 4-ounce turkey breast cutlets

Salt and pepper to taste

3 tablespoons oil

½ cup (1 stick) butter

1 cup plus 2 tablespoons unbleached all-purpose flour

6 cups (1½ quarts) chicken or turkey broth

Chopped fresh sage to taste

Orange-braised Mustard Greens, following

Soak the dried fruits in warm water to cover for 15 minutes; drain and set aside. Preheat the oven to 350°. On a hard surface, pound the turkey cutlets flat with the bottom of a heavy bottle. Spread the mixed fruit evenly on the cutlets and roll them, securing the ends with toothpicks. Season with salt and pepper.

In a sauté pan or skillet, heat the oil, add the roulades, and sauté to brown lightly on all sides. Place the roulades in a baking dish and bake them in the preheated oven for 10 minutes. Remove the roulades from the pan and keep warm.

Melt the butter in the baking pan and stir in the flour over medium heat until it begins to brown; whisk in the stock. Simmer for 25 minutes, stirring occasionally; stir in the sage.

To serve, cut the roulades into slices. On each plate, place a layer of the mustard greens, spoon over some of the sauce, and arrange the turkey roulade slices in a pinwheel shape on top.

Makes 12 servings

ORANGE-BRAISED MUSTARD GREENS

2 pounds young mustard greens

3 tablespoons unsalted butter

1 cup chopped shallots

1 cup fresh orange juice

Salt and pepper to taste

In a large pot of boiling salted water, blanch the mustard greens for 3 minutes; drain. In a sauté pan or skillet, melt the butter over medium-high heat and sauté the shallots until translucent. Add the mustard greens, orange juice, salt, and pepper and simmer for 10 minutes, or until most of the liquid has evaporated. Serve warm or at room temperature.

Makes 12 servings

Saxon Plum Pudding with Armagnac Coulis

⅓ cup pitted prunes

⅓ cup Armagnac

½ cup blanched almonds

½ cup (1 stick) unsalted butter, at room temperature

6 eggs, separated

3 ounces (3 squares) semisweet chocolate, finely grated

½ cup sugar

Armagnac Coulis, following

Place the prunes in a small bowl, pour Armagnac over, and soak for 30 minutes. Drain, reserving the liquid. Mince the prunes. Whirl the almonds in a blender until they are finely ground. Preheat the oven to 325°. In a large bowl, beat the butter until creamy. Beat in the egg yolks one at a time until thoroughly blended. In another bowl, combine the chocolate, almonds, and prunes. Add this mixture to the egg yolk mixture and blend; set aside.

In a large bowl, beat the egg whites, adding the sugar gradually, until they form stiff peaks. Fold the egg whites into the egg yolk mixture. Lightly butter and sugar 12 individual (1½-cup) soufflé dishes and fill them equally with the pudding mixture. Bake in the preheated oven for 40 minutes, or until puffed and firm. To serve, unmold the puddings upside down on a large serving platter and pour the Armagnac *coulis* around them.

Makes 12 servings

Armagnac Coulis

2 cups prunes

Reserved Armagnac soaking liquid from Saxon Plum Pudding, preceding

¼ cup sugar

½ cup canned prune juice

1 teaspoon freshly grated lemon zest

1 teaspoon freshly grated orange zest

¼ cup Armagnac

In a blender or a food processor, purée the prunes with the soaking liquid. In a medium saucepan, place the prune purée and all the other ingredients and cook until the mixture is reduced by about one fourth. Serve warm.

Granola Yogurt Parfait with Minted Rhubarb Compote

½ cup water

1 cup sugar

4 teaspoons plain gelatin

3¾ cups (30 ounces) plain lowfat yogurt

2½ cups granola

Minted Rhubarb Compote, following

Fresh mint leaves for garnish

In a medium saucepan, bring the water to a boil; add the sugar, cook for 1 minute, and remove the pan from the heat. Add the gelatin, stirring until it's completely dissolved, then place the mixture in the refrigerator to chill.

When the gelatin mixture is chilled, whisk it into the yogurt, then add the granola, mixing until thoroughly blended. Rinse 12 custard cups with water and fill them with the yogurt mixture. Refrigerate the parfaits overnight.

To serve, unmold the parfaits onto individual dessert plates, and surround each parfait with ¼ cup of minted rhubarb compote. Garnish with fresh mint leaves.

Makes 12 servings

MINTED RHUBARB COMPOTE

2 cups fresh orange juice

½ cup dry white wine

1 cup water

2 cups sugar

2 pounds rhubarb, cleaned and cut into ½-inch pieces

1 cinnamon stick

1 bay leaf

1 teaspoon ground cloves

1 teaspoon ground allspice

½ cup chopped fresh mint

In a large saucepan, bring the orange juice, wine, water, and sugar to a boil and cook for 5 minutes. Add the rhubarb, spices, and mint and cook for 10 minutes longer. Chill before serving.

T·H·E ❀ C·L·O·I·S·T·E·R®

The Cloister is a Five-Star, Five-Diamond world-class resort set amid lush gardens on Sea Island off the coast of Georgia. The resort includes five miles of beach, historic sites, and ten thousand acres of protected forests and serene marshes. Spanish Mediterranean architecture was used for the original buildings of the main hotel, while the River House and more recent building additions reflect the eaves and roof lines of the Caribbean.

Recreational activities at the resort include golf, tennis, swimming, skeet, riding, boating, fishing, bicycling, lawn sports, strolling the gardens, and dancing as well as winter programs in bridge, cooking, wine, tennis, and golf. The formal dining in the hotel's main dining room is acclaimed, but there is also casual dining at the beach and golf clubs, cookouts, and plantation suppers. Famed big bands make the Cloister America's foremost resort for ballroom dancing.

The Holidays are very special at the Cloister when the halls are decked, the grounds lighted, and children are engaged in holiday adventures and parties of their own. The hotel's traditional Yule log ceremony, candlelight Christmas feast, and holiday music and dancing are enjoyed tremendously. The following menu was created by the Cloister's sous chef, William Still.

THE CLOISTER
MENU

Serves Twelve

Blue Crab Bisque Altamaha

Butter Lettuce with
Goat Cheese and Lemon-Walnut Oil Vinaigrette

Squash Soufflé Frederica with
Vidalia Onion Coulis

Blueberry Spoom Savannah

Green Beans with Country-smoked Bacon

Georgia Quail Stuffed with
Wild Rice, Pecans, and Wild Mushrooms
with Bourbon Shallot Sauce

Golden Isles Meringue with Peach Concasse

Blue Crab Bisque Altamaha

1 cup (2 sticks) butter

1 cup flour

4 cups (1 quart) Fish Stock, page 231, or clam juice

2 cups (1 pint) heavy cream

½ medium onion, finely diced

1 celery stalk, finely diced

½ leek, white part only, finely diced

Salt, white pepper, and paprika to taste

4 ounces lump blue crab meat

4 ounces claw blue crab meat

¾ cup dry sherry

1 bunch fresh chives, chopped, for garnish

In a 1-gallon stockpot, heat ¾ cup (1½ sticks) of the butter over medium heat, then stir in the flour to make a roux. Cook the roux for 5 minutes, then add the fish stock, stirring constantly. When the mixture thickens and begins to boil, lower the heat, add the cream, and simmer for 5 minutes.

In a small sauté pan or skillet, heat 2 tablespoons of the butter and sauté the vegetables until they are tender. Add the salt, pepper, and paprika and stir into the simmering soup base in the stockpot. In the sauté pan, heat the remaining 2 tablespoons of the butter and sauté the crab meat; season. Add ¼ cup of the sherry to the crab and cook for 5 minutes. Add the crab meat to the stockpot and adjust the seasoning. To serve, fill soup bowls two-thirds full, then add 2 table-spoons of sherry to the top of each portion. Sprinkle with chives.

Makes 6 to 8 servings

Note: This recipe is named after the Altamaha River, near Savannah. Blue crabs are abundant in southeast Georgia.

Butter Lettuce with
Lemon-Walnut Oil Vinaigrette

VINAIGRETTE

1 egg

1 teaspoon salt

4 teaspoons ground white pepper

1 tablespoon sugar

2 cups walnut oil

2 tablespoons red wine vinegar

¼ cup fresh lemon juice

2 tablespoons minced celery

2 tablespoons minced walnuts

Leaves from 3 heads butter lettuce

3 ounces goat cheese

In a large bowl, whisk the egg until frothy. Add the salt, white pepper, and sugar; gradually whisk in the walnut oil. Blend in the vinegar and lemon juice, and fold in the celery and walnuts.

Divide the lettuce leaves among 6 to 8 salad plates. Crumble the goat cheese over the lettuce, and refrigerate until needed. Just before serving, spoon some dressing over the salad, as desired.

Makes 6 to 8 servings

Squash Soufflé Frederica with Vidalia Onion Coulis

1 tablespoon clarified butter, page 231

1 medium Vidalia onion, diced

1 pound yellow squash, cut into ½-inch-thick slices

Salt and white pepper to taste

½ cup heavy cream

3 eggs

1 red bell pepper, cored, seeded, and diced

1 green bell pepper, cored, seeded, and diced

Vidalia Onion Coulis, following

Preheat the oven to 350°. In a sauté pan or skillet, heat the butter and sauté the onion until translucent. Add the squash, season to taste, and continue cooking until the squash is tender. Strain, reserving the liquid for the onion coulis, and place the onion and squash in a blender or food processor; purée. With the motor running, gradually blend in the cream until smooth, then add the eggs and continue blending just long enough to mix. Turn the motor off and fold in the diced peppers; correct the seasoning.

Butter the sides of six 3-by-2-inch soufflé molds. Fold the squash mixture into the molds, then place them in a 9-by-13-inch baking pan with ½ inch of water in the bottom. Bake in the preheated oven for 15 to 25 minutes, or until a toothpick inserted into the center of a soufflé comes out clean. Unmold the soufflés on individual serving plates with the onion *coulis* spooned around the bottom. Serve warm.

Makes 6 servings

Note: Frederica is the name of a fort on St. Simon's Island, Georgia. It was built around 1730 by James Oglethorpe to defend the colony against the Spanish. Vidalia onions, available in some gourmet food stores and specialty markets, are sweeter than yellow onions and are named after a town in eastern Georgia.

Vidalia Onion Coulis

2 tablespoons butter

3 medium Vidalia onions, diced

Salt and white pepper to taste

½ cup Sauterne, or other sweet white wine

1 cup reserved liquid from squash soufflé, or chicken broth

In a 10-inch sauté pan or skillet, heat the butter and sauté the onions until translucent. Add the salt, pepper, white wine, and the reserved liquid or chicken broth, and cook until the liquid is reduced by two thirds. Transfer to a blender or food processor and purée.

Blueberry Spoom Savannah

1 envelope (1 tablespoon) plain gelatin

1 cup sugar

1½ cups water

2 cups (1 pint) fresh or thawed frozen blueberries

2 tablespoons fresh lemon juice

2 egg whites

Holly or blueberry sprigs for garnish

In a saucepan, combine the gelatin, sugar, and water and cook over medium heat until the gelatin and sugar dissolves. Add the blueberries and lemon juice and cook for 5 minutes more; transfer to a blender or food processor and purée. Pour the mixture into a container and place in the freezer, stirring every 10 minutes until slushy.

In a large bowl, whip the egg whites until they form soft peaks. Fold in the fruit mixture, then return to the original container and freeze again, stirring occasionally until frozen. To serve, scoop the spoom into wineglasses, and serve on plates garnished with a holly or blueberry sprig.

Makes 6 to 8 servings

Note: Spoom is a Southern word for a sorbet or frozen dessert; this recipe is intended to be used as a palate cleanser.

Green Beans with Country-smoked Bacon

5 cups water, lightly salted

1 pound green beans

6 slices country-smoked bacon

Preheat the oven to 350°. In a stockpot, bring the water to a boil and blanch the beans for 5 to 7 minutes. Place in a bowl of ice water to cool. In a sauté pan or skillet, cook the bacon until it is translucent but not browned; place on paper towels to drain. Divide the green beans into 6 portions and wrap each bundle with bacon, using a toothpick to hold the ends of the bacon together. Heat in the preheated oven for 10 to 12 minutes, or until the bacon is crisp.

Makes 6 servings

Georgia Quail Stuffed with
Wild Rice, Pecans, and Wild Mushrooms Stuffing

1 bacon slice, diced

2 shallots, diced

½ cup wild rice

Salt and pepper to taste

1 cup chicken broth

1 tablespoon butter

4 ounces wild mushrooms (chanterelle, oyster, shiitake, or white)

½ cup broken pecan halves

2 tablespoons bourbon

½ boneless chicken breast, tendons and fat removed

¼ cup heavy cream

1 egg

6 boneless quail

6 bacon slices

1 to 2 tablespoons butter, melted

Bourbon Shallot Sauce, following

Preheat the oven to 350°. To make the stuffing: In a sauté pan or skillet, sauté the bacon until crisp, about 5 to 7 minutes. Add 1 of the shallots, the wild rice, salt, pepper, and ¾ cup of the chicken broth. Reduce the heat, cover, and simmer until the rice is done, about 40 minutes, adding more chicken broth if needed.

In another sauté pan or skillet, heat the butter and sauté the mushrooms and the remaining shallot until the shallot is translucent. Add the pecans and half of the bourbon and cook for 3 minutes, then remove from the heat and set aside. Coarsely chop the chicken breast, then place it in a blender or a food processor and chop fine. With the motor running, add the cream, egg, and the remaining bourbon, blending until smooth. Transfer to a bowl and fold in the wild rice and sautéed mushrooms and pecans until thoroughly mixed. Let cool.

When cool, form the stuffing into six 2-inch balls. Place a quail over each ball, skin side up, with the breast on top. Form each quail around the ball, and place the legs in an upward position. Wrap a bacon strip around the bottom, and secure the ends with a toothpick. Place the stuffed quail in a baking pan and brush them with melted butter. Bake in the preheated oven for 20 to 25 minutes, or until the quail are a rich brown color. Serve with bourbon shallot sauce.

Makes 6 servings

Bourbon Shallot Sauce

½ cup (1 stick) unsalted butter, cut into pieces

3 shallots, diced

½ cup bourbon

½ cup chicken broth

½ cup heavy cream

In a sauté pan or skillet, melt 1 tablespoon of the butter and sauté the shallots until translucent. Add the bourbon and reduce. Add the chicken broth and cream and reduce again, simmering to reduce the total volume by one third. Remove from the heat and gradually whisk in the remaining butter.

Golden Isles Meringue with Peach Concasse

3 egg whites

⅛ teaspoon salt

⅓ cup sugar

2 cups milk

PEACH CONCASSE

4 cups (1 quart) water

3 peaches

4 tablespoons butter

¼ cup brown sugar

⅓ cup peach brandy or cointreau

In a large bowl, whisk together the egg whites and salt until frothy. Gradually add the sugar and continue whisking until the egg whites form stiff peaks. In a medium saucepan, bring the milk to a simmer. Drop spoonfuls of meringue into the milk and poach for 2 to 3 minutes, turning once. Remove the meringues with a slotted spoon and place on plates; refrigerate.

To make the *concasse*, place the water in a large saucepan and bring to a simmer. Gently place the peaches in the water and cook for 3 to 5 minutes. Transfer the peaches to a bowl of ice water. When cool, peel the peaches, cut them in half, and remove the pits. Dice the fruit into ⅜-inch cubes.

Arrange the meringues on dessert plates. In a sauté pan or skillet, melt the butter and stir in the brown sugar. When this mixture begins to bubble, stir in the peaches. Add the brandy or cointreau, heat, and set on fire with a match. Pour over the meringues and serve immediately.

Makes 6 to 8 servings

Note: The Golden Isles—including Sea Island, home of the Cloister— line the Georgia coast.

The Hotel del Coronado is a National Historic Landmark, the world's largest wooden structure, and the largest full-service beachfront resort on the North American Pacific Coast. This magnificent Victorian American seaside hotel from the 1880s is painted white and topped with a bright red roof featuring an enormous rotunda.

Guests at the resort enjoy the beach, tennis, swimming, surfing, fishing, boating, and golfing. San Diego's wonderful climate is perfect for the exotic plants of the hotel's beautiful central courtyard and grounds. The Hotel del Coronado has completed an extensive restoration project and is now one of Southern California's largest and most successful meeting and convention facilities.

The hotel's Crown Room, with its thirty-three-foot sugar pine ceiling, has been the setting for huge state dinners for presidents, princes, and heroes. The room is used for elegant evening dining, the hotel's exceedingly popular Sunday brunch, and holiday dining. The following menu is a favorite Christmas dinner menu from the Del Coronado.

Hotel Del Coronado
Menu

Serves Six

Winter Squash Soup

Hearts of Romaine, Avocado, and Grapefruit Salad
with Walnut Vinaigrette

Wild Rice Timbales

Glazed Baby Carrots with Water Chestnuts

Sautéed Green Beans with Red Pepper Julienne

Fanned Breast of Duckling with Grand Marnier Sauce

Orange Baskets with Cranberry Relish

Hot Apricot Tarts with Sabayon Sauce

Winter Squash Soup

6 acorn squash

One 14-ounce can pumpkin purée

⅓ cup sugar

⅛ teaspoon *each* ground cinnamon, nutmeg, ginger, cardamom

4 cups (1 quart) half and half

¼ cup anisette liqueur

1 cup plain yogurt

Cut off the top of each acorn squash so that the edge is beveled inward, reserving the top. Scoop out the seeds and pulp with a spoon, being careful not to puncture the base. Place in an oven set at 325° and bake the squash for 10 minutes to dry out the shells.

In a 4-quart pot, combine all the remaining ingredients except the yogurt. Cook over low heat for 30 minutes. Remove from heat and pass the mixture through a food mill or force through a sieve.

Fill each warmed acorn squash with ¾ cup of soup. Serve the squash with the tops on, if desired, and garnish soup with a dollop of yogurt.

Makes 6 servings

Hearts of Romaine, Avocado, and Grapefruit Salad with Walnut Vinaigrette

2 heads romaine

2 medium avocados

2 medium pink grapefruit

Sprigs from 1 bunch watercress

WALNUT VINAIGRETTE

½ cup walnut oil

½ cup cider vinegar

½ cup fresh lemon juice

Salt and pepper to taste

¾ cup chopped walnuts

Trim off the base of each head of lettuce to make the head 5 inches long. Slice the romaine into 3 lengthwise sections. Place each section on a salad plate. Peel and quarter the avocados, then slice each quarter into 4 pieces, making a fan. Place each avocado fan on a bed of romaine.

Peel and section the grapefruit. Place 3 grapefruit sections on one side of each romaine bed and arrange sprigs of watercress on the opposite side.

In a small bowl, mix together the walnut oil, vinegar, and lemon juice. Add the salt and pepper. Spoon vinaigrette over each salad and sprinkle with walnuts.

Makes 6 to 8 servings

Wild Rice Timbales

4 cups (1 quart) warm water

2 cups wild rice

4 tablespoons butter

¼ cup minced onions

5 cups chicken broth

One 2½-ounce can pâté de foie gras

Salt and white pepper to taste

In a large bowl, place the water and rice, soak for 15 minutes, and drain. In a 2-quart saucepan, melt the butter and sauté the onions until golden. Add the chicken broth and bring the mixture to a boil. Add the rice to the broth. Bring the broth to a boil again, then reduce the heat and cover. Simmer for 45 to 50 minutes, or until the rice is tender.

Remove from the heat and allow to cool for 30 minutes. Blend in the pâté; season to taste. Pack the rice mixture into 6 buttered custard cups. Let cool, then run a knife around the inside of each timbale and invert to unmold onto serving plates.

Makes 6 servings

Glazed Baby Carrots with Water Chestnuts

12 baby carrots

3 tablespoons butter

¼ cup brown sugar

One 3-ounce can water chestnuts, drained and sliced

Trim and peel the carrots, leaving ⅛ inch of green stems. In a saucepan, parboil the carrots in boiling water to cover until al dente, about 7 or 8 minutes; drain off the water. Add the butter and brown sugar to the carrots and heat until the butter is melted. Add the water chestnuts to the carrot mixture.

Makes 6 servings

Sautéed Green Beans with Red Pepper Julienne

1 pound green beans

6 tablespoons butter

1 medium red bell pepper, cored, seeded, and cut into julienne

Salt and white pepper to taste

Parboil the green beans in boiling water to cover until al dente; drain. Cool the beans under cold running water; drain. In a sauté pan or skillet, melt the butter and sauté the beans until heated through. Add the bell pepper and stir rapidly for 1 minute. Add salt and pepper.

Makes 6 servings

Fanned Breast of Duckling with Grand Marnier Sauce

Six 12-ounce duck breasts

¾ cup orange marmalade

Salt and white pepper to taste

Grand Marnier Sauce, following

Orange Baskets, following

Preheat the oven to 350°. Place a wire rack on a baking sheet. Roll each duck breast tightly, tie with cotton strings, and place on the wire rack. Lightly season with salt and pepper and bake in the preheated oven for 25 minutes. Remove from the oven, remove strings, drain off fat, and glaze the duck with the marmalade. Increase the oven temperature to 450° and return the duck to the oven to roast for an additional 10 minutes. Remove from the oven and let cool to room temperature.

Slice each breast into 5 or 6 pieces and fan out in the center of a dinner plate. Top with Grand Marnier Sauce and garnish with an orange basket.

Makes 6 servings

GRAND MARNIER SAUCE

2 cups sugar

⅔ cup fresh orange juice

⅓ cup Grand Marnier

In a heavy saucepan, cook the sugar, stirring, over low heat until it turns a light brown; be careful not to burn the sugar. Add the orange juice and Grand Marnier. Cook and stir over low heat until the sauce is smooth and thickened.

ORANGE BASKETS WITH CRANBERRY RELISH

6 small Valencia oranges

½ cup fresh cranberries

1 apple, peeled and coarsely chopped

1 lemon, coarsely chopped

1 lime, coarsely chopped

1 cup sugar or to taste

½ cup canned cranberry sauce

To make the orange crowns: Using a sharp knife, cut off the top off each orange so that the edge is serrated. Remove the orange pulp with a spoon or juicer, discard the juice, and place the hollowed-out crowns aside. Place the orange pulp and all the remaining ingredients into a blender or a food processor. Chop coarsely. Taste and add more sugar if the mixture is too tart. Fill the orange crowns with the cranberry relish.

Hot Apricot Tarts with Sabayon Sauce

One 20-ounce can apricot halves in heavy syrup

2½ tablespoons sugar

2 tablespoons apricot brandy

½ tablespoon arrowroot

1 tablespoon cold water

6 ounces frozen puff pastry dough, defrosted

Sabayon Sauce, following

Drain the canned apricots, reserving the juice. In a saucepan, place the apricot juice, sugar, and apricot brandy. Bring the mixture to a boil. Mix the arrowroot with the water and slowly whisk into the boiling mixture. Reduce the heat to a simmer. Add the apricot halves and cook for 5 minutes.

Preheat the oven to 350°. Roll out the puff pastry dough to make a 9-inch square about ¼ inch thick. Cut into three 3-by-3-inch squares. On a large baking sheet covered with parchment or greased with butter, place the pastry squares and bake in the preheated oven until golden brown, about 8 minutes. Allow the pastry to cool, then lift off the top half of each square. Spoon some of the hot apricot mixture onto each pastry shell and top with sabayon sauce. Serve immediately.

Makes 6 servings

SABAYON SAUCE

4 egg yolks

½ cup sugar

½ cup Marsala wine

1 tablespoon orange liqueur

In a double boiler, beat together the egg yolks and sugar. Cook over medium heat, stirring constantly, until the mixture begins to thicken. Gradually blend in the wine and liqueur. Keep warm over very low heat.

CHICAGO

T he Drake is a Chicago landmark and is listed in the National Register of Historic Places. It was constructed in 1920 by architect Ben Marshall for John and Tracy Drake. The hotel features a classical facade, floors of Tennessee marble, and a structure of solid Bedford limestone. Important interior architecture includes the Cape Cod Room and the famous Gold Coast Room. WGN's first radio broadcasts were aired from atop the Drake while famous big bands played in the Gold Coast Room. Banquets for Queen Elizabeth II of England, Emperor Hirohito of Japan, opening night receptions, and casual dinners of every sort have been celebrated at the hotel. The Drake has undergone an extensive renovation and has been restored to its original splendor.

The hotel's immensely popular Cape Cod Room serves Chicago's most extensive seafood menu. It has consistently been named one of America's top restaurants and has won the Holiday Award for thirty-four years.

Award-winning Executive Chef Leo Waldmeier, who believes that dining "should be a total experience which melds food and atmosphere to an essence of one," created this romantic new Year's Eve dinner for *Menus and Music*.

THE DRAKE
MENU

Serves Six

Tart Niçoise

Pheasant Consommé with Five-Star Anise

Lobster Salad with Mango Sauce

Steamed Salmon with Cilantro and Fresh Ginger

Noisettes of Lamb with Goat Cheese

Raspberry Yogurt Delight with Raspberry Coulis

Tart Niçoise

4 medium eggplants, cut lengthwise into ½-inch-thick slices

4 zucchini, cut into ¼-inch slices

4 teaspoons chopped garlic

Salt and pepper to taste

½ cup olive oil

2 bunches basil, stemmed and roughly chopped

¼ cup chopped oil-cured black olives

6 tomatoes, peeled and cut into large cubes

Light a wood or charcoal fire in an open grill. Sprinkle the eggplant and zucchini slices with garlic, salt, and pepper. Over a low fire, grill the eggplant and zucchini on both sides, using a grill basket. Preheat the oven to 375°.

Line the bottom of two 9-inch pie pans with the eggplant slices; then cover with a layer of basil leaves and half of the black olives. Arrange the tomatoes evenly on top of the basil leaves and cover with the rest of the olives. Season with salt, pepper, and a touch of garlic. Arrange the zucchini in a fan shape on top and bake in the preheated oven for 25 minutes, or until lightly browned.

Makes two 9-inch tarts

Note: This recipe can be prepared 1 day in advance and reheated when ready to serve.

Pheasant Consommé with Five-Star Anise

4 small pheasants (about 2¼ pounds each)

2 celery stalks, sliced

2 medium carrots, peeled and sliced

1 small onion, sliced

Green part of 2 small leeks, sliced

20 peppercorns, roughly crushed

2 small bay leaves

2 teaspoons chopped fresh thyme

Two five-star anise

4 egg whites

4 quarts very rich chicken stock or reduced chicken broth, chilled

Salt and pepper to taste

4 tablespoons butter

Use a boning knife to remove the breast meat from the pheasants. Remove and discard the skin and trim any fat or membranes from the breast meat; then cover tightly and refrigerate. Chop the rest of the birds into small pieces.

In a stockpot, place the pheasant pieces, celery, carrots, onion, leeks, peppercorns, bay leaves, thyme, and star anise. In a large bowl, whisk together the egg whites and 2 cups of the cold chicken stock. Add this mixture to the stockpot with the remaining chicken stock and blend thoroughly.

Bring to a simmer over medium-low heat. As soon as the stock begins to simmer, reduce the heat so that only an occasional bubble floats to the surface. Do not stir or in any way disturb the foamy crust that floats on the stock, or the consommé will not be clear. Cook uncovered for 3½ hours. Carefully remove the crust and ladle the soup gently through a muslin-lined sieve. (You should have about 9 cups of consommé.) Allow the consommé to cool, then cover and refrigerate.

At serving time, skim off all fat particles and heat the consommé in a saucepan over low heat. Set 12 shallow soup plates in a warm oven to heat. Season the pheasant breast pieces with salt and pepper. In a medium sauté pan or skillet, melt the butter over medium heat, add the pheasant meat to the pan, and sear for about 7 minutes, turning once; the meat should be medium rare. Place the pheasant pieces between paper towels for 5 minutes.

To serve, cut each piece of breast meat in long, narrow slices and arrange in a fan in a heated soup plate. Immediately ladle the hot consommé over each and serve at once.

Makes 12 servings

Note: The excellence of this intense consommé depends on the quality of the stock, which should be strong and fat-free. This dish can be prepared 1 day in advance.

Lobster Salad with Mango Sauce

Four 1½-pound live lobsters

6 mangoes, peeled and pitted

1½ cups mayonnaise

Juice of 1 lime

Juice of 1 orange

1 tablespoon curry powder

3 tablespoons vodka

Salt and freshly ground pepper to taste

1 cup shredded fresh coconut

1 cup alfalfa sprouts

Kill the lobsters by plunging a knife in at the point where the body meets the tail. Plunge the lobsters into a large pot of rapidly boiling salted water and cook them for 7 minutes. Allow the lobsters to cool in the water. Remove the meat from the shells; remove the sandbag, intestinal vein, and spongy lungs. Cut the meat into large cubes and refrigerate. (The lobsters can be cooked 1 day in advance.)

In a blender or a food processor, purée 2 of the mangoes until smooth; then spoon the puréed fruit into a bowl. Add the mayonnaise, lime and orange juices, curry powder, vodka, salt, and pepper and mix well.

Cut the remaining mangoes into thin slices and arrange on chilled salad plates. Place the lobster meat on top of the fruit; then top with the mango sauce and coconut. Garnish with small bunches of alfalfa sprouts.

Makes 12 servings

Steamed Salmon with Cilantro and Fresh Ginger

2½ cups bean sprouts

2½ cups snow peas

2½ cups julienne-cut carrots

2½ cups julienne-cut shiitake mushrooms

2½ cups julienne-cut leeks

Twelve 5-ounce salmon steaks, about 1 inch thick

2 tablespoons minced fresh ginger

3 tablespoons minced fresh cilantro

2 tablespoons minced garlic

¼ cup soy sauce

2½ teaspoons Asian sesame oil

2½ cups chicken broth

1 cup dry white wine

10 green onions, chopped

Salt and pepper to taste

Preheat the oven to 425°. Place the vegetables in a baking pan. Place the salmon steaks on top of the vegetables. In a mixing bowl, thoroughly combine all the remaining ingredients; then sprinkle this mixture over the salmon steaks and vegetables. Cover the pan tightly with aluminum foil and bake in the preheated oven for 20 minutes.

Note: This dish can be prepared 1 day in advance, then reheated before serving.

Makes 12 servings

Noisettes of Lamb with Goat Cheese

One 5-pound boneless rack of lamb

6 ounces goat cheese

6 ounces natural cream cheese

1 egg yolk

1 tablespoon minced fresh thyme

1 tablespoon minced fresh rosemary

2 garlic cloves, minced

Salt and pepper to taste

Vegetable oil

Lamb Demi-Glace, following

Preheat the oven to 425°. Cut the rack of lamb into 24 medallions. In a bowl, combine the cheeses, egg yolk, herbs, and garlic, mixing thoroughly. Add salt and pepper.

Season the lamb medallions with salt and pepper. In a sauté pan or skillet, heat enough oil to coat the bottom of the pan until very hot; then brown the lamb medallions quickly on both sides. Place the medallions in a baking pan and top each with a tablespoon of the cheese mixture. Bake in the preheated oven for 6 to 7 minutes, or to preferred doneness. Serve on a pool of lamb demi-glace.

Makes 12 servings

LAMB DEMI-GLACE

½ cup vegetable oil

4 pounds lamb bones, cut into small pieces

1 onion, diced

2 carrots, peeled and diced

2 celery stalks, diced

2 tablespoons tomato paste

2 cups dry red wine

4 garlic cloves

1 bay leaf

1 teaspoon chopped fresh rosemary

Salt and pepper to taste

Preheat the oven to 450°. Place the oil in a heavy baking pan and heat on top of the stove. Add the lamb bones and brown them in the oven. When the bones are beginning to brown, add the diced vegetables and tomato paste; then continue baking until the bones are brown.

Transfer the lamb bones to a stockpot. Discard the fat in the baking pan and pour in the red wine; cook and stir over medium heat. Pour this liquid over the bones; add the garlic, bay leaf, and rosemary, and simmer until the wine is reduced to one third its original amount. Add water to cover and gently simmer for 3 hours. Strain through a fine sieve and add salt and pepper.

Makes 2 cups

Raspberry Yogurt Delight with Raspberry Coulis

32 ounces plain yogurt

24 ounces raspberry yogurt

4 cups (1 quart) heavy cream

3 egg yolks

1 cup sugar

2 envelopes (2 tablespoons) gelatin

½ cup cold water

1 cup fresh raspberries

RASPBERRY COULIS

2 cups fresh raspberries, or one 10-ounce package frozen unsweetened
   raspberries, defrosted

Powdered sugar to taste

1 tablespoon kirsch, or to taste

In a large bowl, combine the yogurts, cream, egg yolks, and sugar, blending until smooth; set aside. In the top of a double boiler, soak the gelatin in the cold water for 5 minutes, then cook over boiling water until dissolved. Pour into the yogurt mixture, stirring gently.

Pour a shallow layer of the yogurt mixture into a 9-by-12-inch Pyrex dish, then add a layer of raspberries. Continue adding layers until all of the raspberries are used, ending with a layer of yogurt. Place the terrine in the refrigerator to set for at least 5 hours.

To make the *coulis*: In a blender or a food processor, place the 2 cups fresh raspberries, powdered sugar, and kirsch, and purée until smooth.

To serve, place the dish in a tray of hot water for a few minutes, then run a wet knife around the edges. Carefully turn the dish upside down on a baking sheet. Cut in slices with a warm knife and serve immediately on dessert plates, covered with raspberry *coulis*.

Makes 12 servings

Hotel duPont
WILMINGTON, DELAWARE

The Hotel duPont opened its doors in 1913 when Pierre S. duPont decided to provide lodgings for visitors to Wilmington, Delaware, who were conducting business with his company. DuPont's affinity for opulence is evident in the hotel's grand Italian Renaissance-style architecture with its travertine marble wainscoting, carved walnut and oak paneling, and coffered gold-encrusted ceilings patterned after the Doges' Palace in Venice.

Today guests of the Hotel duPont enjoy the nearby Winterthur Museum and Gardens, the Delaware Art Museum, the Brandywine River Museum, Longwood Gardens, and the beautiful landscape of the Brandywine Valley. The hotel has an outstanding collection of Brandywine River School art including several Wyeth paintings. The duPont's in-house theater seats twelve hundred and has been the site for performances by Leopold Stowkowski and the Philadelphia orchestra, Sarah Bernhardt, Al Jolson, Fred Astaire, and Joel Grey.

The duPont's celebrated Green Room, with its oak paneling, gilded musician's gallery, and elaborate coffered ceiling, is Wilmington's favorite site for commemorative occasions and culinary events. Distinguished French and American fare is also served in the hotel's Christina and Brandywine rooms. The following holiday dinner was created for *Menus and Music* by the duPont's Executive Chef, Hubert M. Winkler.

HOTEL duPONT
MENU

Serves Twelve

Cream of Pumpkin Soup with Curry

Green Beans with Tomatoes

Spiced Glazed Yams

Roast Turkey with Chestnut and Sausage Stuffing

Cinnamon Parfait with Figs and Cassis

Cream of Pumpkin Soup with Curry

4 tablespoons butter

½ cup chopped onion

3 teaspoons curry powder

6 cups (1½ quarts) chicken broth

32 ounces (4 cups) canned pumpkin purée

¼ cup packed brown sugar

Salt, white pepper, and nutmeg to taste

2 cups heavy cream

Chopped fresh chives or parsley for garnish

In a 6- or 8-quart saucepan, melt the butter over medium-high heat. Add the onion and sauté until translucent. Add the curry powder and cook, stirring, for 2 minutes. Reduce the heat to medium and stir in the chicken broth, pumpkin, brown sugar, salt, pepper, and nutmeg; cook for 10 minutes. Stir in the heavy cream and cook for an additional 5 minutes.

Cook 10 minutes longer for a thick soup, or add more broth if you prefer it thinner. Adjust the seasoning. Pour the soup into a blender or food processor and purée until smooth and creamy. Ladle into bowls and garnish with chives or parsley.

Makes 12 servings

Green Beans with Tomatoes

3 pounds green beans

6 tablespoons butter

1 medium onion, chopped

1½ teaspoons minced garlic

1 teaspoon chopped fresh thyme

4 medium tomatoes, peeled, seeded, and coarsely chopped

Salt and white pepper to taste

In a large pot of boiling salted water, blanch the beans for about 4 minutes. Drain and rinse in cold water to stop the cooking process. (This can be done ahead of time.)

Heat the butter in a sauté pan or skillet. Add the onion and cook over medium heat until translucent; do not brown. Add the garlic, thyme, and tomatoes and cook for 1 minute. Add the green beans and heat thoroughly. Season with salt and pepper and serve.

Makes 12 servings

Spiced Glazed Yams

5 pounds medium yams or sweet potatoes

¾ cup (1½ sticks) butter

½ teaspoon ground allspice

½ teaspoon ground cinnamon

¼ teaspoon ground nutmeg

¼ teaspoon ground ginger

1½ cups maple syrup

1½ cups packed brown sugar

1 teaspoon cider vinegar

Salt and white pepper to taste

Preheat the oven to 400°. Place the yams or sweet potatoes in a baking pan and bake in the preheated oven for 45 minutes, or until tender when pierced with a knife. Remove and let cool. Reduce the oven to 350°. In a medium saucepan, melt the butter. Add the spices and sauté for 1 minute to bring out the flavors. Mix in the syrup and sugar; cook, stirring, until the sugar is melted. Stir in the vinegar. Remove from the heat and add salt and pepper; set aside.

Peel and slice the yams or sweet potatoes and place them in a buttered baking dish. Pour the glaze over them and bake in the 350° oven for 15 to 20 minutes, or until heated through. Serve warm.

Makes 12 servings

Roast Turkey with Chestnut and Sausage Stuffing

1½ pounds chestnuts

One 14-to 16-pound turkey

4 tablespoons butter

2 medium onions, chopped

3 celery stalks, chopped

1½ pounds breakfast sausage

1½ pounds mushrooms, chopped

One 3-pound bag seasoned croutons

2 to 3 cups chicken broth

Salt and pepper to taste

Preheat the oven to 375°. With a sharp knife, cut an X in the flat side of each chestnut. Place the chestnuts on a baking sheet and roast them in the preheated oven for 15 minutes. Shell, then peel off the brown skin with a paring knife. Chop the nut meats and set aside.

Lower the oven temperature to 325°. Wash and dry the turkey inside and out; set aside. In a large saucepan, melt the butter. Add the onions and celery and sauté for 10 to15 minutes, or until lightly browned. Add the sausage, breaking it up as it cooks. Cook the sausage for 10 minutes, or until lightly browned. Add the mushrooms and chestnuts and cook again for 10 minutes. Add the croutons and 2 cups of the chicken broth. Add more chicken broth if necessary to make the stuffing lightly moist. Season with salt and pepper.

Stuff the turkey loosely. Truss the turkey, then place it in a baking pan and roast in the preheated oven for 3 to 3½ hours, or until a meat thermometer registers 180°, basting every 15 to 20 minutes. To test for doneness, prick the thigh with a fork; the juices should run clear.

Makes 12 servings

Cinnamon Parfait with Figs and Cassis

PARFAIT

1¾ cups sugar

18 egg yolks

1½ teaspoons vanilla extract

6 cups (1½ quarts) heavy cream, whipped

¾ cup Frangelica liqueur, or to taste

2 to 3 tablespoons ground cinnamon

SAUCE

12 fresh figs

1¾ cups sugar

2 cups red wine

2 cups cassis (black currant liqueur)

To make the parfait, combine the sugar, egg yolks, and vanilla in a large bowl. Whip at high speed until the mixture is thick and frothy. Fold in the whipped cream and add the Frangelica. Add the cinnamon to taste, a little at a time. Pour into 12 custard cups and freeze overnight.

To make the sauce, place the figs in a medium saucepan. Add the sugar, wine, and cassis. Cook slowly until the figs are tender, about 5 minutes, then remove them from the liquid with a slotted spoon. Continue cooking the liquid for about 10 minutes longer until it thickens to the consistency of syrup; set aside and keep warm. Just before serving, unmold the chilled parfaits by dipping the cups into hot water. Invert onto individual serving plates. Garnish each parfait with 1 warm fig and 2 to 3 tablespoons of the warm syrup.

Makes 12 servings

The Empress

V ictoria's venerable Empress Hotel is one of North America's finest heritage landmarks. As a Canadian Pacific Hotel & Resort, the Empress is in the grand tradition of the Banff Springs Hotel and Chateau Lake Louise.

It is majestically set on the water's edge and across from Parliament on Vancouver Island, British Columbia. The nine acres of beautifully landscaped grounds surrounding the hotel flourish in the temperate climate that has given Victoria its "City of Gardens" name. Charming English architecture and quaint shops, as well some of the world's most exciting salmon fishing and scuba diving, are enjoyed in Victoria.

The Empress has just completed an extensive restoration project that has enhanced the stately beauty of the hotel and updated its hotel services, restaurants, and lounges. The renowned Palm Court, Crystal Ballroom, Bengal Lounge, and Conservatory have been restored. A new swimming pavilion, recreation area, and conference center have also been added.

Afternoon tea in the Empress's lobby or Palm Court is a great attraction for visitors from all over the world, and the Empress Dining Room is especially noted for fine dining in an elegant atmosphere. The following winters eve dinner was created for *Menus and Music* by the Empress's Executive Chef, David Hammonds.

THE EMPRESS MENU

Serves Six

Timbales of Seafood with Saffron and Chardonnay

Artichoke and Hazelnut Soup

Granite of Pink Grapefruit and Mint

Rabbit Stuffed with Vancouver Island Chanterelles

Terrine des Fruits with Strawberry and Kiwi Sauce

Timbales of Seafood with Saffron and Chardonnay

SPINACH PURÉE

½ bunch spinach, stemmed

1 tablespoon water or white wine

1 pound fresh scallops

¾ cup heavy cream

Salt and pepper to taste

1 pound fresh shrimp, shelled and deveined

12 ounces fresh salmon, skinned and boned

SAUCE

2 tablespoons butter

2 tablespoons chopped shallots

½ cup Chardonnay

Pinch of saffron

3¼ cups heavy cream

3 tablespoons brandy

Salmon caviar and chopped fresh herbs for garnish

To make the spinach purée: In a medium saucepan, place the spinach and water or white wine and simmer, covered, for 5 minutes, or until no liquid remains. Transfer to a blender or a food processor and purée; set aside.

continued

Place the scallops in a blender or a food processor and purée. Continue to purée while gradually adding ¼ cup of the cream in a steady stream. Add 1 tablespoon of spinach purée and blend (reserve the remaining purée for another use). Season with salt and pepper and refrigerate. Repeat the same method, but do not add the spinach purée, with the shrimp, then the salmon, and refrigerate each separately.

Butter 12 custard cups. Using a pastry bag, pipe a layer of chilled salmon mousse to fill the bottom third of each cup. Fill the second third of each cup with a layer of the shrimp mousse, and then add the salmon mousse to fill each cup. Place the cups on a rack in a large kettle of boiling water and steam for 20 minutes, or until firm (the mousse should spring back when lightly touched in the center).

To make the sauce, heat the butter in a sauté pan or skillet and sauté the shallots until they are translucent. Add the Chardonnay and the saffron and cook to reduce the liquid. Stir in the cream and brandy and cook over low heat, stirring constantly, until the sauce is thickened and smooth. Correct the seasoning.

Just before serving, unmold each timbale by dipping each cup briefly into hot water, then inverting it onto a serving plate. Cover each timbale with sauce and garnish with salmon caviar and fresh herbs.

Makes 12 servings

Artichoke and Hazelnut Soup

½ cup (1 stick) butter

1 pound onions, chopped (about 3 ½ cups chopped)

Four 16-ounce cans artichoke bottoms, drained and chopped

1 ¼ cups unbleached all-purpose flour

4 quarts chicken broth

2 ¼ cups sliced hazelnuts

Salt and pepper to taste

2 cups (1 pint) heavy cream

In a large pot, heat the butter. Add the onions and artichoke bottoms and sauté until the onions are translucent. Stir in the flour and cook for 2 to 3 minutes. Add the chicken broth, 2 cups of the hazelnuts, and seasonings, and cook the soup for 45 minutes.

Pour the soup in batches into a blender or food processor and purée. Return the puréed soup to the pot, add the cream, and adjust the seasoning. Heat through, pour into bowls, and garnish with the remaining ¼ cup sliced hazelnuts.

Makes 12 servings

Granite of Pink Grapefruit and Mint

¾ cup fresh mint leaves

2 tablespoons honey

1 cup dry white wine

One 6-ounce can frozen pink grapefruit juice

Set aside some of the mint leaves for garnish and mince the remaining leaves as finely as possible. In a small saucepan, bring the honey, white wine, and mint to a boil. Add the grapefruit juice. Place in a container and set in the freezer for 3 or 4 hours, stirring it every 30 minutes. To serve, scoop into champagne glasses and garnish with fresh mint.

Makes 12 servings

Rabbit Stuffed with
Vancouver Island Chanterelles

6 whole rabbits

4 tablespoons butter

2½ cups chopped onions

1 pound fresh chanterelles, sliced

½ cup brandy, heated

2 cups (1 pint) heavy cream

Salt and pepper to taste

12 ounces caul fat, or 18 bacon slices blanched in boiling water for 10 minutes, rinsed, and drained

SAUCE

4 tablespoons butter

¼ cup chopped shallots

2 tablespoons green peppercorns

¼ cup Madeira wine

1 cup Veal Stock, page 233

2 cups heavy cream

Salt and pepper to taste

Remove the legs of the rabbits and and debone the legs. Remove the breast from each rabbit in one piece with the belly skin attached.

In a sauté pan or skillet, heat the butter and sauté the onions and chanterelles until the onions are translucent. Pour the brandy into the pan and light it with a match. Remove the pan from the heat and let the mixture cool. Place the rabbit leg meat and the cream in a blender or food processor, in batches if necessary, and purée. Stir the mousse into the sautéed vegetables, and season to taste.

Preheat the oven to 350°. Lay out each rabbit breast and cover it with a layer of mousse. Roll each breast and wrap it in caul fat or 3 bacon slices; tie the rolls closed with cotton string. In a sauté pan or skillet, sauté the stuffed rabbit breasts until they turn light brown. Place the rabbit breasts in a baking dish and bake them in the preheated oven for approximately 15 minutes.

While the rabbit is baking, prepare the sauce. In a sauté pan or skillet, heat the butter and sauté the shallots until translucent. Add the peppercorns and Madeira and cook to reduce the liquid by half. Add the demi-glace. Add the cream and simmer for a few minutes. Correct the seasoning.

Before serving, slice the rabbit rolls and pour the sauce over.

Makes 12 servings

Terrine des Fruits with Strawberry and Kiwi Sauce

2 cups plain yogurt

6 ounces natural cream cheese, at room temperature

¼ cup cold water

2 envelopes (2 tablespoons) plain gelatin

4 egg yolks

½ cup sugar

1 ¾ cups heavy cream, lightly whipped

1 pint fresh strawberries, stemmed and sliced

6 kiwi fruit, peeled and sliced

Strawberry and Kiwi Sauce, following

In a bowl, whisk together the yogurt and cream cheese; set aside. Place the water in the top of a double boiler and sprinkle the gelatin over; let sit for 3 minutes. Place over boiling water and stir to dissolve; set aside. In a large heat-proof bowl set over a pot of simmering water, whisk the egg yolks and sugar together. Remove from the heat and blend in the yogurt mixture. Place the bowl over the hot water to warm through, then remove from the heat and add the gelatin; let cool. Gradually fold in the whipped cream.

Line the bottom and sides of a 6-cup soufflé dish with waxed paper. Pour in one-third of the gelatin mixture and layer the sliced strawberries on top. Add a second layer of one-third of the gelatin mixture and cover with kiwi slices. Cover with the remaining gelatin mixture. Freeze the terrine for 12 hours or overnight. To serve, invert the dish to unmold. Cut 2 thin slices per serving and arrange on a plate with strawberry and kiwi sauce.

Makes 12 servings

STRAWBERRY AND KIWI SAUCE

1 pint strawberries, stemmed

3 kiwi fruit, peeled and chopped

Place the fruit in a blender or a food processor and purée until smooth.

The *Greenbrier*

The Greenbrier is a legendary American resort set in the Allegheny Mountains at White Sulphur Springs, West Virginia. Its healing sulphur springs were discovered in 1778 , and the resort began in the early 1800s as a cottage community surrounding the famous springs. A National Historic Landmark, the Greenbrier has been a recipient of the Mobil Five-Star award for the past twenty eight years and the AAA Five-Diamond Award since its inception. The Greenbrier is a modern full-service resort and conference center with state-of-the-art spa and mineral baths surrounded by sixty-five-hundred acres of gardens, golf courses, and mountain forests. Guests at the resort enjoy a wide variety of sports and social activities to suit every taste or interest. Sport activities include golf, tennis, indoor and outdoor swimming, bowling, bicycling, trap and skeet, riding, hiking, and fishing. In winter, there is cross-country skiing, ice skating, or riding in an old-fashioned horse-drawn sleigh.

The Greenbrier offers tea and chamber music each afternoon and gracious dining in the main dining room which serves Continental and American cuisine. Many of its chefs are graduates of the Greenbrier Culinary Apprenticeship Program. The following menu is from the Greenbrier's Christmas Day dinner menu.

THE GREENBRIER MENU

Serves Twelve

*Smoked Allegheny Mountain Trout with
Creamed Horseradish Sauce*

Essence of Bell Pepper and Rosemary

Waldorf Salad

Dilled Cucumbers

Candied Sweet Potatoes

Brussels Sprouts with Chestnuts

*Traditional Greenbrier Valley Turkey with
Sausage Dressing and Giblet Gravy*

Cranberry Relish

Plum Pudding with Apricot Sauce

Smoked Allegheny Mountain Trout with Creamed Horseradish Sauce

4 cups (1 quart) water

4 tablespoons salt

¾ cup chopped fresh dill

Juice from 2 lemons

12 trout fillets with skin

Horseradish Sauce, following

In a large stainless steel stockpot, combine the water, salt, dill, and lemon juice and stir. Add the trout, cover, and marinate for 15 minutes. Cold-smoke the trout at 160° for 15 to 20 minutes. Remove the skin from the trout, and chill in the refrigerator for 5 hours. Serve with horseradish sauce.

Makes 12 servings

CREAMED HORSERADISH SAUCE

1 cup freshly ground horseradish

1½ cups heavy cream, whipped

1 tablespoon fresh lemon juice

Salt and pepper to taste

In a large bowl, combine all the ingredients.

Makes about 4 cups

Essence of Bell Pepper and Rosemary

1½ red bell peppers

¼ onion, chopped

½ carrot, peeled and chopped

1 celery stalk, chopped

8 egg whites

1 pound lean ground beef

8 cups (2 quarts) chicken broth

2 teaspoons chopped fresh rosemary

Remove the core and seeds from the peppers. Chop 1 pepper, reserving the trimmings. Chop the onion, carrot, and celery. In a stockpot, mix together the vegetables, egg whites, and ground beef. Stir in the chicken broth and rosemary, and slowly bring the mixture to a boil. Reduce the heat and simmer for 1 hour; strain.

Place the pepper trimmings in a piece of cheesecloth and tie it closed with a piece of cotton string. Add to the stockpot. Just before serving, remove the sachet and reheat the essence. Cut the halved red pepper into julienne. Divide the julienne among 12 soup bowls, ladle in the essence, and serve.

Makes 12 servings

Waldorf Salad

6 whole apples

Juice of 1 lemon

¾ cup mayonnaise

¾ cup sour cream

½ tablespoon fresh lemon juice

½ tablespoon sugar

½ teaspoon salt

Pinch ground white pepper

1 cup chopped celery

¾ cup chopped walnuts

12 leaf lettuce leaves

12 walnut halves

24 orange segments

Quarter, core, peel, and slice the apples. Place them in a bowl and mix with the lemon juice; set aside. In a large bowl, combine the mayonnaise, sour cream, lemon juice, sugar, salt, and pepper. Just before serving, add the apples, celery, and walnuts. Serve on a leaf of lettuce and garnish each serving with a walnut half and 2 orange segments.

Makes 12 servings

Dilled Cucumbers

6 large cucumbers, peeled and seeded

3 tablespoons chopped fresh dill

⅓ cup heavy cream

¾ cup plain yogurt

Salt and pepper to taste

Cut the cucumbers into ½-inch slices. In a large bowl, thoroughly combine the cucumbers with all the remaining ingredients. Chill in the refrigerator for 1 to 2 hours.

Makes 12 servings

Candied Sweet Potatoes

6 medium yams or sweet potatoes

4 tablespoons butter

¼ cup honey

1 teaspoon salt

Boil the yams or sweet potatoes in their jackets for 25 minutes, or until tender when pierced with a knife. Preheat the oven to 350°. Peel and slice the sweet potatoes and place them in a buttered baking dish. Meanwhile, in a small saucepan, melt the butter and mix in the honey and salt, stirring until thoroughly blended. Pour the glaze over the yams or sweet potatoes and bake in the preheated oven for 20 minutes, or until heated through.

Makes 12 servings

Brussels Sprouts with Chestnuts

16 chestnuts

2½ pounds Brussels sprouts

½ cup (1 stick) butter

Salt and ground white pepper to taste

Cook the chestnuts in boiling water to cover until they pop open. Shell, then peel off the brown skin with a paring knife; chop the nut meats and set aside.

Blanch the Brussels sprouts in boiling water for 10 to 15 minutes; drain, cool, and set aside. In a sauté pan or skillet, heat the butter until it melts and browns slightly. Add the Brussels sprouts and chestnuts and cook until they are heated through. Season with salt and pepper.

Makes 12 servings

Traditional Greenbrier Valley Turkey with Sausage Dressing and Giblet Gravy

One 20- to 24-pound turkey

Oil

Salt and pepper to taste

Chopped fresh thyme and parsley

Sausage Dressing, following

Giblet Gravy, following

Preheat the oven to 350°. Remove the giblets and the neck from the turkey (reserve them for the giblet gravy) and coat the turkey lightly with oil inside, then season inside with salt, pepper, and half of the herbs. Tuck the wing tips back under the breast, truss the turkey, coat the outside with oil, and season with salt, pepper, and the remaining herbs.

Place the turkey on a rack in a roasting pan. Cook in the preheated oven for 1 hour, then cover the turkey loosely with aluminum foil and cook for an additional 2 hours, or until a meat thermometer registers 180°. Remove the turkey from the oven and allow it to rest at least 20 minutes before carving. Serve with dresssing and giblet gravy.

Makes 12 servings

SAUSAGE DRESSING

14 ounces pork sausage, chopped

1 cup chopped onion

1 cup chopped celery

4 cups coarsely crumbled cornbread

10 cups coarsely chopped French bread or hard rolls

1½ teaspoons poultry seasoning

1½ teaspoons chopped fresh sage

1 teaspoon salt

¼ teaspoon ground white pepper

3 to 3½ cups chicken broth

Preheat the oven to 400°. In a sauté pan or skillet, brown the sausage and drain off the fat. Add the onion and celery and continue cooking until the onion is translucent. Transfer to a mixing bowl and blend in the breads. Add the poultry seasoning, sage, salt, and pepper, and gradually add the chicken broth until the dressing is moist and pasty. Combine thoroughly and transfer to a casserole. Bake in the preheated oven for 30 minutes, or until the dressing is heated through.

GIBLET GRAVY

Turkey neck and giblets

1 large onion, chopped

3 carrots, peeled and chopped

3 celery stalks, chopped

3 tablepoons chopped shallots

Salt to taste

2 tablespoons oil

2 cups dry red wine

8 cups (2 quarts) turkey and chicken broth

½ teaspoon chopped fresh thyme

½ teaspoon chopped fresh sage

3 tablespoons arrowroot, dissolved in ¼ cup water

Port wine to taste (optional)

Place the turkey neck and giblets, 2 tablespoons of the chopped onion, one third of the carrots and celery, and 1 tablespoon of the shallots in a saucepan. Bring to a boil, cover, and reduce heat to a simmer. Cook for 30 minutes. Strain, reserving the giblets, and set the broth aside.

In a large saucepan, heat the oil and cook the remaining onions, carrots, and celery until lightly browned. Add the remaining shallots and cook until they are translucent. Stir in the wine and cook to reduce the liquid by one half. Add the chicken broth to the reserved turkey broth to make 8 cups. Add the broths and herbs to the vegetable-wine mixture and simmer for 1 hour. Stir in the arrowroot and cook until the gravy thickens as desired; then cook for an additional 10 minutes and strain. Chop the reserved giblets and add to the gravy; add the port wine, if desired.

Cranberry Relish

1 orange, coarsely chopped

1 cup water

1½ pounds (1½ bags) fresh cranberries

1 cup sugar

Purée the orange, peel and all, in a blender or a food processor with a little of the water until coarsely ground. Pick over the cranberries and remove any stems or spoiled berries; rinse and drain. In a large saucepan, combine all the ingredients and simmer for 5 minutes, stirring occasionally. Remove from heat and let cool before serving.

Makes about 3 cups

Plum Pudding with Apricot Sauce

1½ cups raisins

1½ cups currants

½ cup citron or mixed candied fruit

½ cup curacao (orange liqueur)

Juice and grated zest of 1 orange

4 ½ cups fresh bread crumbs (about 9 bread slices)

8 ounces (about 2 cups) suet, chopped

½ cup unbleached all-purpose flour

1 cup sugar

½ tablespoon ground cinnamon

¼ teaspoon ground nutmeg

¼ teaspoon ground cloves

Pinch baking soda

3 eggs, slightly beaten

½ cup milk

Apricot Sauce, following

In a large bowl, combine the raisins, currants, and citron. Add the curacao and orange juice and zest and mix well. Cover and let sit overnight.

Preheat the oven to 350°. In a large bowl, thoroughly combine the bread crumbs, suet, flour, sugar, cinnamon, nutmeg, cloves, and baking soda. Blend in the eggs and milk, then fold in the fruit mixture. Pour into buttered molds and place the molds in a baking pan. Pour water into the baking pan to halfway up the sides of the molds. Bake in the preheated oven for 2 hours. To unmold, run a knife around the inside of each mold and invert on a serving plate. Serve with apricot sauce.

Makes 12 servings

APRICOT SAUCE

1 cup canned apricots, with a little of their syrup

1 cup sugar

½ cups water

Juice of 1 lemon

In a blender or food processor, chop the apricots. In a medium saucepan, combine the apricots, sugar, water, and lemon juice. Bring the mixture to a boil and continue cooking for 2 to 3 minutes. Remove from the heat and strain through a fine sieve. Serve hot or cold, as desired.

Halekulani

On the Beach at Waikiki

The Halekulani Hotel, which has been accommodating guests since 1917, brings back the style, elegance, and music of the Hawaiian Islands in the days of steamship travel, when the original Halekulani was one of the few hotels on Waikiki Beach.

The Halekulani, a name meaning "House Befitting Heaven," is a member of Preferred Hotels Worldwide and The Leading Hotels of the World and is the winner of the American Automobile Association's highest rating, the Five-Diamond Award.

The hotel's new design incorporates the restored historic main building of the Halekulani of the 1930s into its five interconnecting buildings. They are surrounded with courtyards and gardens overlooking the Pacific Ocean and Diamond Head. The main building houses the hotel's restaurant, La Mer, winnner of the Travel Holiday Award as well the prestigious Ambassador Award. The restaurant serves fine French cuisine with an island influence. The hotel also has an indoor-outdoor dining room, Orchids, and "The House Without a Key" which was immortalized in an Earl Derr Biggers's Charlie Chan novel. One of the great traditions of the old Halekulani was the ritual of sunset cocktails and Hawaiian music under a towering kiawe tree. Today the century-old tree still stands as a Waikiki landmark and musicians still sing the songs of old Hawaii nearby. The Halekulani's Executive, Chef George Mavrothalassiti, created the following festive Christmas Eve dinner for *Menus and Music*.

HALEKULANI MENU

Serves Twelve

Consommé of Duck with Truffles en Croûte

Salad of Prawns and Smoked Duck with Mesclun

Roasted Goose with Apple Cider and Honey Sauce

Crottins de Chavignol Rôti

Chocolate Yule Log with Raspberry Filling

Consommé of Duck with Truffles en Croûte

Two 4- to 5-pound ducks

16 cups (1 gallon) cold water

Salt to taste

2 large carrots

1 turnip

2 leeks

3 celery stalks

1 onion

1 bay leaf

3 thyme sprigs

GARNISH

3 carrots, peeled

3 celery stalks

3 leeks, white part only

3 truffles

⅓ cup fresh chervil leaves

6 frozen puff pastry sheets, defrosted

5 egg yolks

¼ cup water

Debone the ducks and remove the fat from the legs and meat; set the breast meat aside for the Salad of Prawns and Smoked Duck with Mesclun (page 120). In a large stockpot, place the duck bones, meat, and cold water. Bring to a boil and skim off the foam thoroughly. Add the salt, carrots, turnip, leeks, celery, onion, and herbs. Cover the soup and simmer for 4 hours. Skim off the fat with a large spoon and strain the broth through a colander lined with muslin or cheesecloth; set aside at room temperature.

continued

Preheat the oven to 375°. Cut the carrots, celery, leeks, and truffles into fine dice. Mix with the chervil. Place 12 deep heatproof soup bowls on a baking sheet. Pour the consommé into the bowls, then sprinkle with the vegetable garnish. Cut the puff pastry into 12 circles 2 inches larger in diameter than the soup bowls. In a small bowl, beat together the egg yolks and water and brush the egg wash on one side of the puff pastry. Set each circle over a soup bowl and slash the top of each circle several times with a sharp knife. Brush the top of each pastry with the egg wash. Bake in the preheated oven for 12 minutes, or until the pastry is golden brown.

Makes 12 servings

Salad of Prawns and Smoked Duck with Mesclun

GARLIC BUTTER

⅓ cup chopped shallots

⅓ cup chopped fresh parsley

⅓ cup chopped garlic

1½ cups (3 sticks) butter, at room temperature

Salt and white pepper to taste

SHERRY VINEGAR DRESSING

½ cup hot water

Salt, white pepper, and cayenne to taste

1 cup sherry vinegar

3 small shallots, chopped

3 garlic cloves, chopped

¼ cup chopped fresh basil

3 cups olive oil

⅓ cup olive oil

48 large prawns (18 to 20 prawns per pound), peeled and deveined

8 ounces *mesclun* (mixed baby greens)

3 smoked duck breasts, boned and skinned

To prepare the garlic butter, combine the shallots, parsley, garlic, and butter in a blender or a food processor and purée. Season with salt and pepper and refrigerate.

To make the sherry vinegar dressing: In a ceramic bowl, mix together the water, salt, pepper, and cayenne. Add the sherry vinegar, shallots, garlic, and basil. Add the olive oil and mix thoroughly.

In a large nonstick sauté pan or skillet, heat the olive oil over medium-high heat and sauté the prawns just until they turn pink evenly. Remove the pan from the heat and add the garlic butter, mixing with a spatula. In a large bowl, toss the mesclun with the sherry vinegar dressing and mix in the slices of smoked duck. To serve, place some of the smoked duck and mesclun mixture in the center of individual salad plates and arrange the prawns around the duck, pouring some of the garlic butter over the prawns. Serve immediately with the remaining garlic butter.

Makes 12 servings

Roasted Goose with Apple Cider and Honey Sauce

4 cups (1 quart) cider vinegar

4 cups honey

Salt, white pepper, and cayenne to taste

Three 8-pound Canadian geese

1 dozen Granny Smith apples, peeled, cored, and halved

6 cups dry white wine

1¼ cups sugar

12 baby bok choy, cut in half

3 cups chicken broth

1½ cups (3 sticks) fresh butter, cut into pieces

Salt and pepper to taste

Preheat the oven to 325°. In a large bowl, combine 3 cups of the vinegar, 1 cup of the honey, and the salt, pepper, and cayenne. Place the geese on racks in a large baking pan and prick all over with a fork. Glaze the geese with the honey mixture and bake for 2 to 2½ hours in the preheated oven, or until juices from the thigh run clear when pierced or a meat thermometer reads 180°. Spread more of the remaining honey mixture over the geese after each 30 minutes of cooking. Remove from the oven and set aside.

Increase the oven temperature to 350°. Place the apples in a baking pan with half of the white wine and the sugar. In another baking pan, place the bok choy with the remaining white wine, the broth, and seasoning. Place both pans in the oven and bake for 15 minutes.

Meanwhile, to prepare the sauce, remove the geese from the pan and remove the grease from the pan drippings with a large spoon and then by laying a paper towel over the surface. Place the baking pan over low heat on top of the stove and pour in the remaining 1 cup of vinegar. Add the remaining 3 cups of honey and cook over low heat until caramelized; be careful not to let the mixture burn. Add any remaining honey glaze, and gradually whisk in the butter. Season to taste and keep warm. Serve the geese with the baked apples and bok choy, accompanied with the sauce.

Makes 12 servings

Crottins de Chavignol Rôti

12 baguette slices

6 crottins de Chavignol, halved, or six 2-ounce slices aged goat cheese

Sesame seeds for sprinkling

12 small grape clusters

Preheat the oven to 350°. On a baking sheet, place the baguette slices and bake in the oven until lightly toasted. Place a piece of cheese on each slice of bread, then sprinkle with sesame seeds. Bake for 8 minutes, or until the cheese is slightly melted.

To serve, arrange the toasts on serving plates and garnish with the grapes.

Makes 12 toasts

Chocolate Yule Log with Raspberry Filling

CAKE

10 eggs, separated

1⅓ cups sugar

2½ cups sifted cake flour

FILLING

1⅓ cups raspberry jam

GANACHE

2 cups heavy cream

1 pound semisweet chocolate, chopped

Christmas candies, cookies, or chocolates for garnish

Preheat the oven to 325°. To make the cake: In a large bowl, place the egg yolks and 1 cup of the sugar. Beat until the mixture is thick and pale in color. Stir in the flour gradually and mix until smooth; set aside.

In a second large bowl, beat the egg whites until soft peaks form. Blend in the remaining ⅓ cup sugar, then fold this mixture gradually into the flour mixture.

Pour the batter evenly on a jelly roll pan that has been greased or lined with parchment paper. Bake in the preheated oven for twelve minutes, or until springy to the touch. The cake will be very lightly colored. Invert the cake onto a dampened kitchen towel, remove the parchment paper if you have used it, and beginning with a long side roll up the cake in the towel. Let the cake cool in the towel. The cake may be made 4 hours in advance and kept wrapped in the towel at room temperature. Unroll the cake partially, being careful not to open it so far that it cracks, and spread the inside of the roll evenly with the jam. Reroll the cake carefully, removing the towel, and transfer the cake roll to a cake board or platter.

To make the ganache: In a saucepan, place the cream over medium-high heat. Bring the cream to the scalding point and remove from the heat. Stir in the chocolate and continue to stir until the mixture has cooled and has reached spreading consistency.

Cut off each end of the cake diagonally with a serrated knife to give the appearance of a sawed log. Spread the ganache over the cake in a rough pattern and run a fork through the frosting to simulate tree bark. Garnish the log with candies and/or cookies of your choice. Slice crosswise to serve.

Makes 12 servings

The Hay-Adams Hotel

Washington, D.C.'s Hay-Adams Hotel is located on Lafayette Square overlooking the White House. Few hotels in the world can boast such proximity to power, for as one writer noted after a visit to the Hay-Adams, it's "as close as one can get to staying at the White House, short of being invited by the President." The Hay-Adams calls itself "an island of civility in a sea of power."

The site has long been a Washington focal point. In 1864, lots on the square were purchased by two young men, statesman John Hay, Lincoln's private secretary and later secretary of state, and historian and writer Henry Adams, the great-grandson of John Adams. They built adjoining residences, which became centers of Washington society. In 1927, the houses were bought and demolished, and the land became a site for a hotel named the Hay-Adams House. The only privately held parcel of real estate on Lafayette Square, the hotel was bought in 1983 by David H. Murdock. For the next two years the hotel underwent extensive renovations.

Today the hotel's Adams Room is called "the location of choice for power breakfasts" by the _Washington Post._ The oak paneling and ornate carved ceiling of the John Hay Room add to the Tudor atmosphere of the dining room. The Hay-Adams's chef, Harry Simpson, created the menu and recipes for the following New Year's Eve dinner served in the John Hay Room.

THE HAY-ADAMS
MENU

Serves Six

Lobster Consommé with Oyster Ravioli

*Smoked Salmon and Lobster Roulade with
Beetroot Vinaigrette*

Red and White Wine Sorbet

*Venison Medallions with
Mustard seed and Horseradish*

Artichoke Flans

Pear-Cassis Soufflé Glace

Lacy Orange Tuiles

Lobster Consommé with Oyster Ravioli

Three 1¼-pound live lobsters

¼ cup olive oil

5 carrots, peeled and diced small

4 onions, diced small

1 celery stalk, diced small

6 parsley sprigs

4 cups (1 quart) dry white wine

8 cups (2 quarts) water

3 tomatoes, seeded and minced

1 leek, white part only, minced

2 tarragon sprigs

4 egg whites

Salt and pepper to taste

3 pieces gold leaf

Oyster Ravioli, following

Minced fresh chives

Kill the lobsters by plunging a knife in at the point where the body meets the tail. Cut the tails from the bodies, then cut the bodies in half lengthwise and remove the claws. Remove the sandbag, intestinal vein, and spongy lungs.

continued

In a large stockpot, heat the olive oil over high heat and sauté the lobster pieces for 2 minutes. Add half of the carrots, all of the onions and celery, 4 of the parsley sprigs, and the white wine. Cook until the wine is reduced by two thirds. Add the water and simmer for 20 minutes, removing the lobster tails after 2 minutes; reserve the tails for Smoked Salmon and Lobster Roulade (page 132). Strain the bouillon through a sieve and let cool.

In a bowl, mix the remaining carrot and parsley sprigs, two thirds of the tomatoes, the leek, and the tarragon with the egg whites. Add this mixture to the cooled bouillon, set over low heat, and simmer for 25 minutes. Ladle the broth through a fine sieve lined with cheesecloth. Return the broth to the stockpot and season with salt and pepper to taste.

Heat the consommé and drop in the gold leaf; whisk gently. Ladle the consommé into 6 soup bowls. Add 3 ravioli to each bowl, along with the zucchini and carrot balls. Sprinkle with the remaining tomatoes and the chives.

Makes 6 servings

Oyster Ravioli

1 yellow zucchini

1 green zucchini

1 carrot

2 tablespoons cognac

½ cup heavy cream

18 oysters, shelled

Salt and pepper to taste

3 egg yolks

¼ cup milk or water

36 wonton wrappers

8 fresh chives, minced

Cut the zucchini and carrot into balls using a very small (No. 10) melon ball scoop; set aside.

In a sauté pan or skillet, boil the cognac for 2 or 3 minutes to burn off the alcohol. Add the cream and boil to reduce the liquid by half. Remove from the heat, add the oysters, and season to taste; set aside.

In a small bowl, beat together the egg yolks and milk or water and set aside. Spread 18 of the wonton wrappers out on a flat work surface. Spoon 1 oyster onto each wonton. Brush the edge of each with the egg wash and cover with one of the remaining 18 wrappers, pressing the edges together to seal. Use a small cookie cutter to cut out smaller circles for ravioli.

In a stockpot, bring a large amount of lightly salted water to a boil. Poach the ravioli with the zucchini and carrot balls for 3 minutes. Remove the ravioli and vegetables with a slotted spoon.

Smoked Salmon and Lobster Roulade with Caviar, Sour Cream, and Beetroot Vinaigrette

DRESSING

1 medium beet

1 teaspoon Dijon mustard

2 teaspoons champagne vinegar

1 teaspoon fresh lemon juice

½ cup extra-virgin olive oil

Salt and pepper to taste

1 pound thinly sliced Norwegian smoked salmon

10 ounces cream cheese, at room temperature

2 tablespoons chopped fresh cilantro leaves

3 lobster tails

⅔ cup sour cream

3 ounces Osetra caviar

6 fresh dill sprigs, for garnish

Cook the beet in boiling water to cover for 30 to 45 minutes, or until tender when pierced with a knife. Drain, cool, and peel. Chop the beet coarsely and purée very briefly in a blender or a food processor so that it is coarsely ground. In a bowl, combine the dressing ingredients with the beet and set aside.

Lay the sheet of overlapping smoked salmon slices out on a sheet of plastic wrap. Blend the cream cheese and cilantro together and spread it onto the smoked salmon. Roll the salmon into the shape of a sausage and refrigerate for 2 hours, or until firm.

Use the cooked lobster tails reserved from the recipe for Lobster Consommé, page 129, or cook the lobster tails in boiling salted water to cover for 12 minutes; drain and cool. Peel and cut the lobster tails into 12 rounds.

To serve, slice the smoked salmon roulade into 12 equal slices. Spoon a generous amount of dressing onto each of 6 salad plates, and place 2 slices of lobster tail and 2 rounds of roulade onto the center of each plate. On top of the lobster, place a teaspoon of sour cream, then place a dollop of caviar on top of the sour cream. Garnish with a sprig of fresh dill.

Makes 6 servings

Red and White Wine Sorbets

SORBET SYRUP

1¼ cups sugar

2⅔ cups water

¼ cup corn syrup

1 bottle dry red wine

Juice of 1 lemon

1 lightly beaten egg white

1 bottle dry white wine

6 strawberry slices and 6 fresh mint leaves for garnish

To make the sorbet syrup: In a saucepan, combine the sugar, water, and corn syrup and bring to a boil, stirring occasionally. Boil the mixture for 3 minutes, skimming the surface if necessary, and remove from the heat. Pass the syrup through a fine sieve and set it aside to cool completely.

After the sorbet syrup has cooled completely, prepare the red wine sorbet. In a large bowl, combine half of the syrup and all the red wine, stirring with a spatula. Add half of the lemon juice and half of the egg white and mix well. Pour the mixture into an ice cream maker and freeze according to the manufacturer's instructions.

To make the white wine sorbet, repeat the process using the white wine. Serve the sorbet in well-chilled martini or champagne glasses, placing a small scoop of red wine sorbet on the bottom and white wine sorbet on top. Garnish with a slice of strawberry and a mint leaf.

Makes 6 servings

Venison Medallions with
Mustard Seed and Horseradish

6 ounces wild mushrooms

1 tablespoon vegetable oil

3 tablespoons butter

1 garlic clove, chopped

2 shallots, chopped

Salt and pepper to taste

Eighteen 2-ounce (1-inch-thick) venison medallions, cut from the loin
  (see Note, page 200)

3 tablespoons mustard seed

½ cup veal or beef stock

½ cup dry red wine

Chopped fresh parsley

1 cup shredded fresh horseradish for garnish

Artichoke Flans, following

If the mushrooms are small, leave them whole; otherwise, cut them in half. In a
sauté pan or skillet, heat 1 teaspoon (one third) of the oil over medium-high
heat. Add the mushrooms and sauté until the juice has evaporated, then add 1
tablespoon of the butter, the garlic, shallots, salt, and pepper. Mix well and continue cooking until everything is lightly browned; set aside.

continued

Season the medallions with salt and pepper. On a work surface covered with a cloth, crack open the mustard seed with the bottom of a skillet and dip the venison medallions into the mustard seed. In a second sauté pan or skillet, heat the remaining 2 teaspoons of oil over high heat. Sauté the medallions on one side for 1 minute; then turn the medallions, add the remaining 2 tablespoons of butter, and sauté for another minute. Remove the venison from the pan, reserving the pan and juices. Add the red wine and stock to the venison juices. Boil to reduce by one third and add the chopped parsley.

To serve, arrange the venison medallions in the center of 6 warmed dinner plates. Scatter the sautéed mushrooms over them, then pour the sauce over. Scatter with horseradish. Unmold the artichoke flans by running a knife around the edge of each one and inverting the cup. Place 1 flan on the side of each plate.

Makes 6 servings

ARTICHOKE FLANS

4 fresh large artichokes

3 large eggs

3 egg yolks, beaten

2 cups heavy cream

1½ teaspoons salt

2 teaspoons rosewater

1 teaspoon sugar

Preheat the oven to 375°. Cut all the leaves and stems from the artichokes and scoop out the chokes with a spoon. In a large saucepan, cook the artichoke hearts and stems in salted boiling water to cover for 10 to 15 minutes or until tender; drain. In a blender or a food processor, purée the artichokes. Strain the purée through a fine sieve set over a bowl; set aside.

In a large bowl, combine the whole eggs, yolks, cream, salt, rosewater, and sugar; beat until foamy. Fold the egg mixture into the artichoke purée and pour into 6 buttered custard cups. Set the cups in a baking dish and pour water into the dish to come halfway up the sides of the cups. Place the dish in the preheated oven and bake for 20 minutes, or until set.

Pear-Cassis Soufflé Glace

3 pears, peeled, cored, and halved

1½ cups water

1½ cups sugar

Juice of ½ lemon

1 cinnamon stick

6 egg yolks

½ cup sifted powdered sugar

1½ pints vanilla ice cream, softened

1½ cups heavy cream, whipped

⅓ cup cassis compound (see Note) or cassis (black currant) liqueur

Berries for garnish

In a medium saucepan, combine the water, sugar, lemon juice, and cinnamon stick and bring to a boil, stirring constantly. Add the pears, reduce heat, and simmer for 20 minutes. Remove the pears with a slotted spoon and transfer to a blender or a food processor; purée and set aside.

In a large bowl, place the egg yolks and powdered sugar and whisk them until the yolks are pale and thick. Add the vanilla ice cream and whisk until fluffy. Fold in the whipped cream. Divide the mixture in half. In one portion, blend in the puréed pears, and in the other the cassis compound.

Fit 6 individual (1 cup) soufflé molds with waxed-paper collars extending 2 inches above the rim of each mold; fasten with paper clips or tape. Fill the molds with the cassis-flavored mixture first, then top with pear-flavored mixture, filling to about 1-¾ inches above the rim. Freeze overnight. Before serving, remove the paper collars. Garnish with the remaining whipped cream and the fresh berries.

Makes 6 servings

Note: Cassis compound is a Swiss black currant syrup available in some gourmet markets.

Lacy Orange Tuiles

¾ cup almonds

¼ cup sifted powdered sugar

¼ cup flour

2 tablespoons fresh orange juice

Grated zest of ½ orange

6 tablespoons butter, melted and cooled

Sifted powdered sugar for sprinkling

In a bowl, combine the almonds, sugar, and flour. Stir in the orange juice and grated zest. Work in the butter, blending until smooth. Cover the bowl and refrigerate for 2 hours.

Preheat the oven to 400°. Grease a baking sheet. Using a soup spoon, spoon 18 mounds of the mixture onto the baking sheet, placing the mounds 2 inches apart. Dip a fork into a glass of cold water and press down lightly on each mound to make a thin pancake about 2 ¾ inches in diameter, dipping the fork in water to make each tuile.

Bake in the preheated oven for about 5 minutes, or until golden brown. Allow to cool for 1 minute. Working quickly, slide a metal spatula under each tuile, then wrap it loosely around the handle of a wooden spoon. Place the tuiles on a serving platter and sprinkle with powdered sugar.

Makes 18 tuiles

THE HEATHMAN HOTEL

The Heathman Hotel, built in 1927 during Portland's greatest growth period, has been listed in the National Register of Historic Places. The ten-story Italian Renaissance-style brick building has been extensively renovated. The lobby, with its handsome gumwood paneling, graceful stairway, and ornate wrought-iron railing, was preserved and restored during the project. Reopened as a luxury hotel in 1984, the Heathman is quite involved in the arts community of Portland. The hotel has a wonderful collection of American art and is located next to the city's new Performing Arts Center.

The Heathman's dining room serves a seasonally varied menu, distinguished by its wide selection of Pacific Northwest seafood and game. The room's award-winning wine list features an extensive selection of Northwest wines. Executive Chef George Tate presented the following dinner menu to *Menus and Music*.

THE HEATHMAN HOTEL
MENU

Serves Six

*Oregon Troll King Salmon Mousse with
Smoked Salmon Sauce*

Pumpkin Cheddar Beer Soup with Cheddar Croutons

Kings Arms Tavern Baked Stuffed Sweet Potatoes

Vineyard Carrots

Roast Wild Goose with Dried Apricot Sauce

Off-the-Cob Relish

Green Tomato Relish

Pepper Relish

Pickled Cauliflower, Carrots, and Mushrooms

Pickled Eggs

Buttermilk Pie

Oregon Troll King Salmon Mousse

1 pound fresh salmon, skinned, boned, and coarsely chopped

1 teaspoon salt

¼ teaspoon ground white pepper

1 slice white bread, trimmed of crusts and cut into cubes

1 egg white

¼ cup heavy cream

½ cup pecans, crushed

Smoked Salmon Sauce, following

2 ounces smoked salmon, diced, for garnish

Chill the salmon thoroughly. Preheat the oven to 350°. Place the salmon in a blender or a food processor and purée. With the motor running, add the salt, pepper, and bread cubes. Add the egg white and blend. Pour the mixture into a bowl and set it in a larger bowl of ice water; fold in the cream and pecans.

Pour the mousse into 6 buttered custard cups and set them in a large baking dish. Pour water into the dish to halfway up the sides of the cups. Place the dish in the preheated oven and bake for 30 to 40 minutes, or until completely set in the center. Remove and let cool. Run a knife around the inside of each mousse and invert to unmold on a serving plate. Spoon the salmon sauce over each mousse and garnish the plate with diced smoked salmon.

Makes 6 servings

SMOKED SALMON SAUCE

½ cup double-strength Lapsang Souchong tea

½ cup heavy cream

1 pound butter at room temperature, cut into pieces

White pepper to taste

continued

In a saucepan, boil the tea rapidly to reduce by half. Add the heavy cream and reduce again until thick. Remove from the heat and gradually beat in the butter. Add pepper and strain through a sieve. Set aside and keep warm over very low heat.

Pumpkin Cheddar Beer Soup

2½ cups chicken broth

2½ cups dark beer

Three 2-pound pumpkins

3 tablespoons butter

3 celery stalks, diced (about 1 cup)

½ leek, white part only

⅔ to ¾ cup heavy cream

2¼ pounds Cheddar cheese, shredded

Cheddar Croutons, following

Place the chicken broth and beer in a kettle over high heat to bring to a boil. Meanwhile, cut the pumpkins into sections, removing the seeds and pith. Cut off the rind, and cut the flesh into medium dice. Cut the leek into medium dice. In a stockpot, heat the butter and sauté the celery and leek until the leek is translucent. Add the pumpkin and sauté for 2 or 3 minutes. Add the boiling broth and beer to the vegetable mixture. Bring to a boil, then reduce the heat and simmer until the pumpkin is tender, about 30 minutes.

Remove the vegetables from the kettle with a slotted spoon to a blender or a food processor and purée in batches, adding liquid as necessary. Return the purée to the liquid and reheat. Stir in the cream and simmer for 5 minutes. Remove from the heat and add the cheese, stirring until it has melted and the mixture is smooth. Serve at once, sprinkled with croutons.

Makes 6 servings

CHEDDAR CROUTONS

8 ounces processed Cheddar cheese, at room temperature

2 tablespoons heavy cream

2½ cups (5 sticks) chilled butter

4 cups unbleached all-purpose flour

3 egg yolks

2 tablespoons chopped fresh parsley

3 tablespoons cold water

½ cup grated romano cheese

In a large bowl, blend together the processed cheese and cream until smooth; set aside. With a pastry cutter or 2 knives, cut the butter into the flour until crumbly. Make a well in the center of the dough and add the egg yolks; mix slightly. Fold in the cheese mixture and the chopped parsley and mix for 1 minute, sprinkling in the water until the consistency of a light pie dough is reached. Add the romano and mix for 30 seconds, or until all ingredients are thoroughly blended.

Transfer the dough to a floured pastry board and knead slightly until firm and smooth. Roll the dough with your palms into a tube shape 2 inches in diameter; wrap in aluminum foil and freeze for several hours.

Preheat the oven to 400° and line a baking sheet with parchment paper or grease with butter. Remove the dough from the freezer, unwrap, and let sit for 5 minutes at room temperature. Slice the dough into ¼-inch-thick rounds and place them on the baking sheet. Bake in the preheated oven for 10 to 12 minutes, or until the croutons lightly brown around the edges.

Makes about 30 croutons

Kings Arms Tavern
Baked Stuffed Sweet Potatoes

¼ cup cranberries

6 medium sweet potatoes or yams

Grated zest and juice of ½ orange

½ apple, peeled, cored, and chopped

½ cup walnuts, chopped

½ cup (1 stick) unsalted butter, melted

1 tablespoon brown sugar, or to taste

Preheat the oven to 400°. Meanwhile, in a saucepan, place the cranberries in water to cover, bring to a boil, and cook until the berries pop open, about 5 minutes; set aside. Place the sweet potatoes or yams in a baking pan and bake in the preheated oven for 45 minutes, or until tender when pierced with a knife. Let cool, cut a slash in the top surface of the sweet potato, and scoop out the pulp; set aside, reserving the shells.

Reduce the oven temperature to 325°. In a large bowl, combine the sweet potato pulp, cranberries, orange juice, apple, and walnuts. Add the butter and brown sugar. Place the mixture in the reserved shells and return them to the oven. Bake until heated through, about 10 to 15 minutes. Garnish with grated orange zest and serve.

Makes 6 servings

Vineyard Carrots

12 medium carrots, peeled

Salt, pepper, and paprika to taste

2 tablespoons butter, melted

⅓ cup cider vinegar, heated

In a saucepan, simmer the carrots in water to cover until tender, about 20 minutes; drain. Cut the carrots lengthwise in quarters and place in a heated shallow serving dish. Season with salt, pepper and paprika, and glaze with melted butter. Pour the hot vinegar over the carrots and serve.

Makes 6 servings

Roasted Goose with Dried Apricot Sauce

One 8- to 10-pound goose
Salt and pepper to taste

MIREPOIX
1 cup chopped onion
½ cup chopped carrot
½ cup chopped celery

GOOSE GLACE
6 cups (1½ quarts) Veal Stock, page 233, or beef broth
Reserved *mirepoix,* above
1 teaspoon tomato paste
1 cup dry white wine

Dried Apricot Sauce, following

Preheat the oven to 400°. Prick the goose lightly with a fork all over and season with salt and pepper; set aside. In a small bowl, mix the onion, carrot, and celery and place the *mirepoix* in a roasting pan (this will keep the goose from sticking). Place the goose on a rack and set it in the roasting pan. Bake in the preheated oven for 30 minutes.

Remove the goose from the oven and lightly prick the skin again to allow any excess fat to drain. Lower the heat to 350° and place the goose back in the oven. Cook 1½ to 2 hours or longer, depending on the size, or until the juices run clear when a thigh is pierced or a meat thermometer registers 180°. Remove from the roasting pan, reserving the pan and the *mirepoix,* and let sit while preparing the goose glace.

Spoon off as much fat as possible from the roasting pan without removing the *mirepoix* and place the pan over medium heat. Pour ½ cup of the veal stock or beef broth into the pan and stir, then cook until the mixture is thick. Stir in the tomato paste. Place in a large saucepan and add the white wine. Boil rapidly to reduce to a thick glaze. Add the remaining veal stock or beef broth and bring to a boil; reduce again to make 2 cups. Strain. Prepare the dried apricot sauce and serve with the goose.

Makes 6 to 8 servings

Dried Apricot Sauce

4 cups (1 quart) dry white wine

1 tablespoon juniper berries

1 tablespoon coriander seeds, crushed

1 tablespoon white peppercorns, crushed

3 cinnamon sticks

1 cup sugar

1½ pounds dried apricots

Goose Glace from Roasted Goose, above

1 cup heavy cream

1 tablespoon cornstarch mixed with 2 tablespoons water

2 tablespoons butter

In a saucepan, place the white wine, spices, and sugar. Bring to a boil, reduce heat, and simmer for 5 minutes. Add the apricots and poach until soft, about 3 minutes. Remove the apricots with a slotted spoon. In a blender or a food processor, purée half of the apricots, reserving the remainder for garnish.

In a saucepan, boil the wine mixture until it is reduced by half. Add the goose glace and boil again until reduced by half. Add the cream and cornstarch paste and boil to reduce the sauce to a consistency thick enough to coat a spoon. Add the apricot purée and simmer for 5 minutes. Blend in the butter and strain through a sieve. Serve warm.

Off-the-Cob Relish

20 medium ears of corn

1½ cups sugar

1 cup diced green bell pepper

1 cup diced red bell pepper

1 cup chopped onion

1 cup diced celery

1 cup brown sugar

1 tablespoon salt

2½ teaspoons celery seed

½ teaspoon turmeric

2½ cups distilled white vinegar

2 cups water

In a kettle, cook the ears of corn in boiling water to cover for 5 minutes. Dip the ears in cold water and cut the corn from the cob. In a kettle, combine the kernels with all the remaining ingredients and simmer for 20 minutes, stirring occasionally. Pour the relish into sterilized jars and process in a boiling water bath (see Note, below). Store in a cool, dry place.

Makes 6 to 7 pints

Note: To sterilize jars and process in a water bath: In a large kettle, sterilize 6 or 7 pint jars in boiling water to cover for 15 minutes. Drain the jars from the hot water just before filling. Fill the jars to 1 inch from the top, making sure the vegetables are covered with liquid. Seal airtight and place on a rack in a large kettle, making sure the jars do not touch. Add water to cover, bring to a boil, and boil for 15 minutes. Remove the jars from the bath with tongs and let cool.

Green Tomato Relish

10 pounds (36 to 40) medium green tomatoes, stemmed, cored, and chopped

¼ cup salt

1¾ pounds onions, chopped

6 green bell peppers, cored, seeded, and chopped

4 red bell peppers, cored, seeded, and chopped

3 cups sugar

6 cups (1½ quarts) cider vinegar

2 tablespoons mixed whole pickling spices

In a large bowl, mix the tomatoes and salt thoroughly. Let stand overnight, then drain off the liquid. Place the tomatoes in a large pot and add the onions, green and red peppers, sugar, and vinegar. Place the spices on a small square of cheesecloth, tie closed with cotton string, and add to the tomato mixture. Boil gently for 1½ hours, or until thickened, stirring frequently.

Remove the spice bag and pour the relish into sterilized jars and process in a water bath (see Note, page 150). Fill the jars to ½ inch from the top and seal air-tight. Store the relish in a cool, dry place.

Makes 8 to 10 pints

Pepper Relish

38 green bell peppers

18 red bell peppers

1 small fresh hot red or green chili

15 red onions, coarsely chopped

2 cups water

5 cups cider vinegar

4 cups sugar

¼ cup salt

5 tablespoons mustard seed

3 tablespoons celery seed

Core, seed, and coarsely chop the bell peppers and chili. Place in a blender or a food processor with the red onions (in batches) and grind, using the finest blade. Place the vegetables in a large ceramic bowl, cover them with boiling water, and let stand for 10 minutes; drain.

In a saucepan, bring the water and 1 cup of the vinegar to a boil. Pour this over the vegetables and let stand for 4 minutes. Drain in a sieve, pressing the vegetables firmly with the back of a large spoon to remove any excess water. Place the vegetables back in the same bowl and add the remaining 4 cups of vinegar and the remaining ingredients, mixing thoroughly. Place the relish in 4 sterilized pint jars and process in a water bath (see Note, page 150). Store in a cool, dry place.

Makes 4 pints

Pickled Cauliflower, Carrots, and Mushrooms

4 cups (1 quart) vinegar

2 tablespoons mustard seed

1 cup sugar

8 whole cloves

4 cinnamon sticks

1 tablespoon mustard seed

1 tablespoon chopped fresh dill

3 pounds carrots

1 cauliflower, broken into florets

3 pounds mushrooms, halved

In a medium saucepan, combine the first 7 ingredients and simmer for 15 minutes. Peel the carrots and cut them into sticks 1 or 2 inches long and ¼ inch thick. Blanch all the vegetables individually in boiling water to cover: Cook the cauliflower for 3 minutes, the broccoli for 2 minutes, the carrots for 4 minutes, and the mushrooms for 1 minute. Let cool. Place the vegetables in 6 to 8 hot sterilized pint jars (see Note, page 150). Strain the hot syrup to remove the spices and pour it into the jar to cover the vegetables; seal airtight and process in a water bath as directed in the note on page 150. Store in a cool, dry place.

Makes 6 to 8 pints

Pickled Eggs

16 hard-cooked eggs

½ tablespoon black peppercorns

½ tablespoon shredded fresh ginger

½ tablespoon whole allspice

4 cups (1 quart) cider vinegar

Pinch of cayenne

Pack the eggs into 3 or 4 hot sterilized wide-mouth pint jars (see Note, page 150). In a saucepan, place the remaining ingredients, bring to a boil, and cook for 10 minutes. Pour the boiling liquid over the eggs. Seal airtight and process in a water bath as directed in the note on page 150. Store in a cool, dry place.

Makes 3 to 4 pints

Buttermilk Pie

1 recipe Pie Pastry, page 232

3 eggs

2 cups buttermilk

1 cup (2 sticks) butter, melted

1 teaspoon vanilla extract

3 tablespoons flour

1 cup sugar

Pinch of salt

Preheat the oven to 450°. Prepare the pastry dough and line a 9-inch pie pan. Crimp the edges and prick the bottom with a fork. Fill with dried beans or pastry weights and bake in the preheated oven for 10 minutes, or until set; set aside.

In a large bowl, whisk the eggs until they are a light lemon color; add all the remaining ingredients and blend well. Pour into the pie shell and bake for 5 minutes at 450°, then reduce the heat to 325°. Bake for 35 to 45 minutes, or until a knife inserted in the center comes out clean.

Makes one 9-inch pie

The Lodge at Vail is a classic Alpine-style chalet in the spectacular Colorado Rockies at the foot of America's largest ski mountain. In winter Vail is a skier's paradise, with more than sixty miles of slopes for all levels of skiing. Guests at the Lodge use ski-lift facilities located just a few steps from the hotel. Ice skating, sleigh rides, and cross-country skiing add variety to winter recreation. The year-round resort community of Vail offers golf, tennis, horseback riding, hiking fishing, and whitewater rafting in a setting of scenic grandeur during the summer.

The Lodge at Vail is a member of The Leading Hotels of the World. It has undergone major improvements to its rooms, public areas, and restaurants under the ownership of VOSE Associated Hotels, the company that restored and runs the famous Venice-Simplon Orient Express Train.

The Wildflower Inn, a Travel Holiday Award-winning restaurant, offers gourmet American dining and an international wine list. Jim Cohen has been the chef of the Wildflower Inn since the restaurant opened in 1984. Chef Cohen created the following winter dinner for *Menus and Music*.

THE LODGE AT VAIL
MENU

Serves Six

Oysters with Cracklings

Lobster Cake with Tomato-Chive Butter Sauce

Field Salad

Lamb Shanks with Garlic Mashed Potatoes

Bread Pudding with Caramel Sauce

Oysters with Cracklings

Skin from 1 whole chicken breast or 2 halves

Pinch of kosher salt

24 oysters in their shell (preferably Catuit or Spinney Creek)

1 shallot, minced

2 tablespoons chopped fresh Italian parsley

Juice of 1 lemon

Ground black pepper to taste

Extra-virgin olive oil for topping

To prepare the cracklings, preheat the oven to 350°. Place the chicken skin on a baking sheet and sprinkle with kosher salt; bake until crisp, about 15 minutes. Remove the skin from the oven, let cool, break it into small pieces, and set aside. Shuck the oysters over a bowl, reserving the liquor. Place each oyster in its deepest shell and arrange them on a plate; distribute the liquor over them. On each oyster, place a pinch of shallot, cracklings, and parsley. Add 2 drops of lemon juice, a little black pepper, and a drop of olive oil to each oyster.

Makes 6 servings

Lobster Cake

½ cup heavy cream

4 slices white bread, trimmed of crusts

12 ounces cooked lobster meat, or one 3-pound lobster, cleaned, cooked, shelled, and diced (see method, page 78)

2 eggs, beaten

1½ tablespoons fresh lemon juice

Salt and pepper to taste

1 tablespoon butter

1 tablespoon oil

Tomato-Chive Butter Sauce, following

In a small saucepan, cook the cream over medium heat, stirring occasionally until the amount of cream is reduced by half; let cool. Preheat the oven to 400°. Tear the bread into pieces and purée in a blender or food processor to make crumbs. Combine the cream, bread crumbs, eggs, lemon juice, and salt and pepper in a large bowl. Shape the mixture into ⅓-cup patties.

In a sauté pan or skillet, melt the butter with the oil and sauté the lobster patties until golden brown. Transfer the patties to a baking sheet and bake in the preheated oven for 5 to 7 minutes. Spoon ¼ cup of the butter sauce with a sprinkling of chives on each of 6 warm plates and place a lobster cake on top.

Makes 6 servings

TOMATO-CHIVE BUTTER SAUCE

7 Roma tomatoes, coarsely chopped

1 bay leaf

5 peppercorns

½ shallot, diced

1 cup dry white wine

2 cups (4 sticks) chilled butter, cut into tablespoons

½ cup chopped fresh chives

Purée the tomatoes in a blender or a food processor. In a large saucepan, place the tomato purée, bay leaf, peppercorns, shallot, and white wine. Cook over medium-high heat until the mixture is reduced by three fourths; remove from heat. Add the cold butter to the tomato mixture a tablespoon at a time, whisking constantly.

Strain through a sieve and return to the saucepan. Keep warm over low heat until serving. After the sauce is pooled on each plate, sprinkle each serving with a heaping tablespoon of chives.

Field Salad

DRESSING

¾ cup olive oil

2 tablespoons balsamic vinegar

Salt and pepper to taste

Leaves from 12 heads baby lettuce or 6 heads Bibb, red leaf,
   or other tender lettuces

6 avocado slices

12 fresh chervil sprigs

In a large bowl, whisk all the dressing ingredients together. Tear the lettuce leaves into pieces and toss with the dressing. Place the tossed leaves on each of 6 salad plates. Place a slice of avocado and 2 sprigs of fresh chervil on each plate.

Makes 6 servings

Lamb Shanks with Garlic Mashed Potatoes

Six 1-pound lamb shanks

Salt and pepper to taste

2 cups unbleached all-purpose flour

About ½ cup olive oil

1 onion, diced

1 carrot, peeled and diced

2 celery stalks, diced

½ fennel bulb, sliced

2 cups dry white wine

6 tablespoons Dijon mustard

1 bay leaf

1 tablespoon peppercorns

1 whole garlic bulb, unpeeled, cut in half

6 cups (1½ quarts) lamb or chicken broth

Preheat the oven to 350°. Season the lamb shanks with salt and pepper and dredge them in the flour. In a sauté pan or skillet, heat half of the olive oil and sear the shanks 2 or 3 at a time until golden brown, adding olive oil as necessary. Transfer the shanks to a heavy ovenproof casserole with a lid, reserving the sauté pan or skillet and its juices. In the sauté pan or skillet, place the onion, carrot, celery, and fennel in the pan juices and sauté until the vegetables are tender. Add the remaining flour and continue cooking until the vegetables turn golden brown. Add the white wine and boil to reduce the mixture by half; then add the mustard, bay leaf, peppercorns, garlic, and broth and bring to a boil.

Pour the vegetable mixture over the shanks, and bake in the preheated oven for about 2 hours, or until very tender, turning the shanks after each 20 minutes of cooking. Remove the shanks from the pan and strain the liquid through a sieve, pressing the vegetables through with the back of a spoon. Place the liquid in a saucepan and cook over medium heat until it is thick enough to coat a spoon.

Correct the seasoning and skim off the fat with a large spoon. Reheat the lamb shanks in the oven and serve with the sauce poured over.

Makes 6 servings

Garlic Mashed Potatoes

6 unpeeled garlic cloves

15 small (1½-inch) unpeeled new potatoes, halved

1 cup heavy cream

½ cup (1 stick) unsalted butter

Salt and pepper to taste

Place the garlic cloves in a baking dish and bake them in a 300° oven for 45 minutes; set aside. In a large saucepan, place the potatoes and add water to cover. Bring to a boil, reduce heat, and simmer until tender, about 15 minutes; drain. In another saucepan, place the cream and butter.

Cut off the ends of the roasted garlic cloves and squeeze the garlic pulp into the saucepan. Heat until the butter is melted; set aside and keep warm. Place the potatoes in a food mill or potato ricer held over a large bowl and purée into the bowl. Stir in the warm cream mixture to blend thoroughly. Add the salt and pepper; serve at once.

Makes 6 servings

Bread Pudding

1 baguette, sliced into rounds

½ cup (1 stick) butter, melted

1½ cups sugar

¾ cup unbleached all-purpose flour

9 eggs

6 cups (1½ quarts) heavy cream

Caramel Sauce, following

Sifted powdered sugar for sprinkling

Preheat the oven to 300°. Place the bread rounds on a baking sheet, brush them with the butter on one side, and bake until golden brown, about 10 minutes. In a large bowl, combine the sugar and flour, then whisk in the eggs and cream until smooth.

In an 11-inch spring-form pan, layer the bread slices. Pour the egg mixture over the bread slices and let sit for 15 minutes. Cover the pan with aluminum foil. Place the pan in a larger baking pan, add hot water to halfway up the sides of the spring-form pan, and bake in the preheated oven for 1 hour. Remove the foil and bake the pudding for another hour; remove from the water bath and let cool. Serve on a pool of caramel sauce and top with more powdered sugar.

Makes 6 servings

CARAMEL SAUCE

½ teaspoon fresh lemon juice

1½ cups sugar

⅓ cup water

1 cup heavy cream

3 tablespoons butter

In a heavy saucepan, combine the lemon juice, sugar, and water. Bring the mixture to a boil, stirring to dissolve the sugar. Cook the syrup over a low heat until it is golden brown, watching carefully to see that it does not burn, then remove it from the heat. Slowly stir the cream into the syrup, then blend in the butter, stirring until a smooth consistency is reached. Set aside and keep warm.

the Mansion on Turtle Creek
DALLAS

T he Mansion on Turtle Creek is Dallas's award-winning luxury hotel and restaurant. It is set amid the four-and-a-half acre estate of the former Sheppard King Mansion overlooking tree-lined Turtle Creek. This 1925 Italian Renaissance-style residence was meticulously restored by Rosewood Hotels in 1982 to house the Mansion on Turtle Creek's restaurant, bar, and private dining rooms. The Historic Preservation League of Dallas gave the hotel an award for renovation and adaptive use of the Sheppard King Mansion. The restaurant's main dining area has a fireplace at each end, a collection of museum-quality art and antiques, original wood paneling, inlaid ceilings, and leaded glass windows. The award-winning Mansion Restaurant features innovative Southwest and American cuisine. Executive Chef Dean Fearing created the following festive menu and recipes.

The Mansion on Turtle Creek Hotel is adjacent to the Sheppard King Mansion. The new nine-story hotel tower has spacious and luxurious hotel guest rooms and suites designed to complement the style of the restored mansion.

THE MANSION ON TURTLE CREEK MENU

Serves Eight to Ten

Tortilla Soup

*Smoked Pheasant Salad with
Ancho-Honey Vinaigrette and Spicy Fried Pasta*

Maple Pecan and Sweet Potato Pie

Tortilla Soup

2 medium onions, coarsely chopped

4 medium tomatoes, coarsely chopped

3 tablespoons corn oil

4 corn tortillas, coarsely chopped

6 garlic cloves, minced

1 tablespoon chopped fresh *epazote* or cilantro

1 tablespoon ground cumin

2 teaspoons chili powder

2 bay leaves

¼ cup canned tomato purée

8 cups (2 quarts) chicken broth

Salt to taste

Cayenne to taste

1 cooked double chicken breast, skinned, boned, and cut into strips

1 avocado, peeled, pitted, and cubed

1 cup shredded Cheddar cheese

3 corn tortillas, cut into thin strips and fried crisp

Place the chopped onions in a blender or a food processor and purée; set aside. Repeat the process with the chopped tomatoes.

Heat the oil in a large saucepan over medium heat. Sauté the tortillas with the garlic and *epazote* until the tortillas are soft. Add the onion and tomato purée and bring to a boil. Add the cumin, chili powder, bay leaves, canned tomato purée, and chicken broth. Bring to a boil again, then reduce to a simmer. Add the salt and cayenne to taste and cook, stirring frequently, for 30 minutes. Skim any fat from the surface.

continued

Strain and pour into warm soup bowls. Garnish each bowl with an equal portion of chicken breast, avocado, shredded cheese, and crisp tortilla strips. Serve immediately.

Makes 8 to 10 servings

Note: Epazote is a Mexican herb sometimes available in Mexican markets.

Smoked Pheasant Salad with Ancho-Honey Vinaigrette and Spicy Fried Pasta

Two 2½-pound pheasants

2 red bell peppers, cored and seeded

2 yellow bell peppers, cored and seeded

2 carrots, peeled

2 small jícamas, peeled

2 small zucchini, quartered lengthwise and seeded

2 teaspoon *each* minced fresh tarragon, parsley, thyme, chives, and basil

2 shallots, minced

2 garlic cloves, minced

¼ cup white wine vinegar

¾ cup peanut oil

Ancho-Honey Vinaigrette, following

Spicy Fried Pasta, following

To prepare the pheasants: In a smoker, burn wood (such as hickory) or wood charcoal down to a gray ash. (Mesquite wood charcoal is the choice at the Mansion on Turtle Creek because it gives the food a true Southwestern character.) Place wood chips or pieces (such as hickory, pecan, apple, or cherry) soaked in water on top of the hot ashes. If the wood chips burn down, add fresh chips to keep the smoke constant. Preheat the oven to 350° while smoking the pheasants for 20 minutes. Transfer pheasants to the preheated oven and cook for about 15 minutes. Cool. (The pheasant can be smoked up to 2 days in advance and refrigerated, tightly covered.)

Remove the skin from the pheasants and cut the breast and thigh meat into fine julienne. Cut the bell peppers, carrot, jícama, and zucchini into fine julienne. In a large bowl, combine the pheasant strips with the bell peppers, carrot, jícama, and zucchini.

In a small bowl, combine the herbs, shallot, garlic, vinegar, and oil. Whisk the mixture until well blended and toss thoroughly with the pheasant mixture to coat all ingredients.

Pool the ancho-honey vinaigrette on 8 to 10 salad plates. Place equal portions of smoked pheasant salad in small mounds in the middle of each plate. Surround each mound with strips of fried pasta.

Makes 8 to 10 servings

ANCHO-HONEY VINAIGRETTE

8 ancho chilies, seeded and cored

4 shallots

4 garlic cloves

2 small bunches cilantro

4 cups (1 quart) water

⅔ cup honey

½ cup white wine vinegar

2 tablespoons balsamic vinegar

1 cup peanut oil

Juice of 1 lime or to taste

Salt to taste

Preheat the oven to 400°. On a baking sheet, place the ancho chilies flat in a single layer. Bake in the preheated oven for 2 minutes. Remove from the oven, allow to cool enough to handle, and peel off the skin.

In a small saucepan, place the anchos, shallots, garlic, cilantro, and water. Bring to a boil and cook for 10 minutes, or until reduced by two thirds. Pour into a blender or a food processor and purée. Add the honey and vinegars, and blend again until smooth. With the motor on, add the peanut oil in a thin, steady stream until all the oil is incorporated. Add lime juice and salt to taste.

Spicy Fried Pasta

2 tablespoons tomato paste

½ tablespoon chili powder

½ tablespoon cayenne pepper, or to taste

1 ½ tablespoons minced seeded jalapeño

½ teaspoon salt

1 extra-large egg yolk

1 teaspoon peanut oil

¼ to ½ cup water

2 cups semolina flour

2 to 3 cups vegetable oil

Combine the tomato paste, chili powder, cayenne pepper, jalapeño, and salt in a blender or a food processor. Blend until smooth. Mix together the egg yolk, peanut oil, and water in a large bowl or a food processor. Add the flour and spice mixture and and blend to make pasta dough according to your pasta machine manufacturer's directions, or stir the ingredients with a wooden spoon or mix with your hands, then form into a ball. Run the pasta through the pasta machine on the thinnest setting or roll out by hand as thin as possible. Cut the pasta into strips about 6 inches long and ⅛ inch wide.

In a deep, heavy pot, heat the vegetable oil to 350°. Deep-fry small amounts of pasta dough at a time for about 45 seconds, or just until crisp. Do not allow the pasta to curl or to turn brown. It should remain straight and bright red. Remove the pasta from the pan with a slotted spoon and drain on paper towels.

Maple Pecan and Sweet Potato Pie

All-Purpose Pastry, following

3 extra-large eggs plus 1 egg yolk

½ cup packed light brown sugar

2 tablespoons unsalted butter, melted

1 teaspoon pure vanilla extract

4½ teaspoons pure maple syrup

1½ cups pecan pieces

2½ cups peeled and cubed sweet potatoes

¼ teaspoon ground ginger

¼ teaspoon ground cinnamon

Pinch of ground cloves

2 egg whites

⅓ cup sugar

½ cup heavy cream, whipped

Prepare the pastry, chill, and roll out to fit a 10-inch flan ring. Line the ring, trim the edges, and set aside.

Preheat the oven to 350°. Combine the eggs, egg yolk, and brown sugar in a medium bowl. Stir until the sugar is dissolved and the mixture is smooth. Blend in the butter, vanilla, and maple syrup until smooth. Sprinkle the pecans evenly over bottom of the pastry shell. Pour the filling into the shell and bake in the pre-heated oven for 30 minutes, or until golden brown. Cool to room temperature.

Meanwhile, place the sweet potatoes in a large saucepan with enough water to cover and bring to a boil over medium heat. Cook for 15 minutes, or until tender; drain. Whip the cooked sweet potatoes with the ginger, cinnamon, and cloves until almost smooth. You should have about 1½ cups of mashed sweet potatoes. Cool in the refrigerator for 20 minutes.

Preheat the oven to 350°. In a large bowl, beat the egg whites until frothy. Gradually add the sugar and continue beating until the whites form stiff peaks. Fold the meringue into the cooled sweet potato mixture.

Gently spoon the sweet potato mixture on top of the pecan pie and smooth the surface. Bake for 20 minutes, or until the filling is firm. Remove from the oven and let cool. Serve at room temperature, garnished with unsweetened whipped cream.

Makes one 10-inch pie

ALL-PURPOSE PASTRY

3 cups unbleached all-purpose flour

1 teaspoon salt

3 tablespoons sugar

1 cup (2 sticks) chilled unsalted butter, cut into pieces

2 extra-large egg yolks, lightly beaten

¼ cup ice water

In a large bowl, combine the flour, salt, and sugar. Cut in the butter with a knife or pastry blender until the mixture resembles coarse meal. Gradually stir in the egg yolks and ice water until a firm dough is formed. Do not overwork the dough. Form the dough into a ball, seal in plastic wrap, and chill for at least 30 minutes.

On a lightly floured surface, roll the dough out to a ⅛-inch-thick circle about 2 inches larger than the pan into which it will be fitted, or cut it into the desired size or shape. Fit the pastry into the pan, trim the edges, and finish as directed.

Makes pastry for one 10-inch double-crust pie

THE POINT

The Point was originally the home of William A. Rockefeller and was the last
and most lavish of the Adirondack Great Camps. Set on New York's
Suranac Lake, the Point continues the tradition of sumptuous Adirondack
retreats by offering guests warm hospitality in a rustic and luxurious atmosphere. It recaptures the gracious lifestyle of a bygone era in a private home, with
eleven distinctive guest quarters that have been beautifully appointed and
meticulously restored by owners Christie and David Garrett.

There are no organized activities at the Point, but guests can explore the
lake in antique boats, hike through the woods, fish, swim, and water ski; play
croquet, badminton, or horseshoes; or enjoy lunch under the pines. Winter
activities include cross-country skiing, skating on the lake, ice fishing, or skiing
the Olympic slopes at nearby Lake Placid.

The resort's Grand Hall, with its enormous stone fireplaces, massive
wood beams, and deep couches, continues the tradition of elegant Great Camp
dining. The imaginative Continental cuisine gains an Adirondack accent from the
use of fresh local vegetables, game, and fish. All dinners and lunches are served
at round tables in the Great Hall unless other arrangements are made. As in a
private home, there is no menu selection, but the fine food and wine always make
meals at the Point a very special event. The inn is especially festive on Thanksgiving and Christmas and serves a resplendent meal for its guests. The following
menu from the Point was presented to *Menus and Music* by Bill McNamee.

THE POINT
MENU

Serves Eight

*Roasted Sea Scallops with Tomato-Sage Coulis
and Cappelletti*

Confit de Canard and Barley Risotto

Wild Turkey with White Truffle and Foie Gras Stuffing

Caprice Cassis

Roasted Sea Scallops with
Tomato-Sage Coulis and Cappelletti

6 sage leaves

1 cup virgin olive oil

4 cups chopped Italian plum tomatoes

Salt and cayenne to taste

5 garlic cloves

Freshly ground black pepper to taste

4 tablespoons butter

40 sea scallops

1 pound *cappelletti*

Fresh-grated Parmesan to taste

In a small saucepan, blanch the sage leaves in boiling water for 10 to 15 seconds. Dip them in a bowl of ice water; pat dry, chop, and set aside.

In a sauté pan or skillet, heat the olive oil over medium heat, then add the tomatoes, salt, and cayenne and cook for 4 minutes. Crush and add the garlic, stir in the sage, and cook for an additional minute, stirring constantly. Add the pepper and adjust the seasonings; set aside. In another sauté pan or skillet, melt the butter and sauté the scallops until golden brown, cooking in batches if necessary. Cook the pasta in a large amount of boiling salted water until al dente. Drain the pasta and place some in the center of each plate. Arrange 5 scallops around the pasta and pour a spoonful of the tomato sauce over. Sprinkle with the Parmesan cheese and serve immediately.

Makes 8 servings

Confit de Canard and Barley Risotto

CONFIT

1 carrot, peeled

1 onion

1 leek

1 celery stalk

8 Moulard duck legs*

4 ½ tablespoons coarse salt

1 bay leaf, crushed

10 cloves

1 head garlic, broken into cloves and peeled

4 pounds fresh duck fat*

BARLEY RISOTTO

2 carrots, peeled

2 celery stalks

2 leeks

2 onions

5 thin slices Parma ham

½ cup duck fat*

1¼ cups barley

2½ cups Duck Stock, page 232

1 bay leaf

Salt and pepper to taste

Preheat the oven to 250°. Coarsely chop all the vegetables and place them in a Dutch oven. Place the duck legs on top of the vegetables. Add the salt, bay leaf, cloves, and garlic, and cover with the duck fat. Cook over low heat until gently simmering, then bake in the preheated oven for 4½ to 5 hours.

To make the risotto, mince the carrots, celery, leeks, onions, and Parma ham. Heat the duck fat in a heavy saucepan and cook the vegetable mixture until tender. Add the barley, duck stock, bay leaf, salt, and pepper. Cover tightly and cook slowly for 1½ hours. Correct the seasonings.

To serve, place 1 serving of risotto in the center of each plate. Top with the duck confit and a little liquid from the risotto.

Makes 8 servings

* Rendered duck fat is available at some specialty meat shops; the Point orders theirs from D'Artagnan in Jersey City, New Jersey (mail orders are available UPS Next Day Air). If desired, you can substitute rendered pork fat. If using pork fat, reduce amount by about one third. Moulard duck legs are available at D'Artagnan.

Wild Turkey with White Truffle and Foie Gras Stuffing

One 15-pound wild turkey*

1 carrot, peeled

½ onion

1 celery stalk

1 bay leaf

Salt and pepper to taste

Chicken broth (optional)

STUFFING

2 celery stalks

1 large onion

2 baby carrots

5 shallots

2 garlic cloves

2 loaves dry French bread, cut into cubes

2 white truffles, chopped

1 fresh uncooked foie gras, chopped*

2 cups turkey broth

2 teaspoons chopped fresh thyme

2 bay leaves

Salt and pepper to taste

Cranberry Relish, page 113

Wash and dry the turkey inside and out; set aside. Chop the carrot, onion, and celery stalk. Place the turkey neck and the giblets in a saucepan and add the vegetables, bay leaf, and salt and pepper. Add water to cover, cover the pan, and simmer for 30 to 45 minutes.

Strain and add chicken broth as necessary to make 2 cups of broth.

Preheat the oven to 350°. To make the stuffing, chop the celery, onion, carrots, shallots, and garlic. In a large saucepan, melt the butter and cook the chopped vegetables until the onion is translucent. Add the French bread, truffles, and foie gras, and cook for 3 minutes, stirring constantly. Stir in the turkey broth, thyme, bay leaves, salt, and pepper. Cover and cook over a low heat for 5 minutes.

Stuff the turkey loosely. Truss the turkey, then place it on a rack in a baking pan and roast in the preheated oven for 3½ to 4 hours, or until a meat thermometer registers 180°. Baste the turkey every 30 minutes while cooking. Serve with cranberry relish.

Makes 8 servings

*Available at some specialty meat shops; the Point orders theirs from D'Artagnan in Jersey City, New Jersey (mail orders are available UPS Next Day Air).

Caprice Cassis

SPONGE CAKE

5 eggs

1 cup sugar

½ cup (1 stick) butter, melted

1 cup sifted cake flour

1 envelope (1 tablespoon) plain gelatin

⅔ cup créme de cassis (black currant liqueur)

1 cup black currants

3 egg yolks

6 tablespoons sugar

2 teaspoons dried milk

1 teaspoon vanilla extract

1 tablespoon water

2 egg whites

1 cup heavy cream

To make the cake, preheat the oven to 375°. Beat together the eggs, sugar, and butter with an electric mixer for 10 minutes. Sprinkle the flour over the egg mixture ¼ cup at a time and fold it in carefully. Pour the batter into a 10-inch tube pan. Bake for 25 to 30 minutes, or until the top is golden and a toothpick inserted near the center comes out clean. Place the pan on a rack and allow the cake to cool completely.

Sprinkle the gelatin over the créme de cassis and let sit. In a blender or a food processor, purée the black currants until smooth; set aside.

In a large bowl, beat the egg yolks for 1 minute, then whisk in 2 tablespoons of the sugar. In a saucepan, combine the cassis *coulis* and dried milk and bring to a boil over medium-high heat; then add to the egg yolk mixture, whisking constantly. Return to the saucepan and heat over low heat until thick enough to coat the back of a spoon. (Do not let the sauce come to a simmer.) Remove from the heat and whisk in the gelatin, créme de cassis, and vanilla extract. Pass the mixture through a sieve and cool.

In a small saucepan, bring the water and the remaining 4 tablespoons of sugar to a boil and cook until a drop of the mixture forms a soft ball in ice water. In a large bowl, whisk the egg whites until they form stiff peaks, then gradually add the hot sugar mixture, whisking until the meringue cools.

In a deep bowl, lightly whip the cream and fold in the cassis mixture and the meringue. Spoon the mousse on top of the sponge cake in the tube pan, and chill in the refrigerator for 5 hours. To serve, run a knife around the edge of the mousse, carefully unmold the cake, and cut in slices.

Makes 8 servings

RAINBOW.

In striking up the twelve-piece Rainbow Room Dance Band in 1987, the revitalized Rainbow Room reentered the life of New York for dining, dancing, and romancing. Since its debut, the Rainbow Room has epitomized New York style, glamour, and sophistication. It opened its doors in 1934 as a skyscraper supper club with two-story-high ceilings, muted colored lights beaming across a domed ceiling (which gave the room its name), and a revolving dance floor. Today, dining at the Rainbow Room is still a theatrical experience: waiters in pastel tails, tableside preparation of classic and contemporary cuisine, and dancing to the Rainbow Room Dance Band. The following recipes for dinner were created by the Rainbow Room's chef, André René.

The Rainbow Room has been rebuilt and restored along with a series of rooms on the sixty fourth and sixty fifth floors of the RCA building. The character of Rockefeller Center is reinterpreted on these two floors to recapture the unique vernacular of American Modernism.

Sharing the top floor with the Rainbow Room is the Rainbow Promenade, a little meals restaurant and bar with views of the Empire State Building, the World Trade Center, and the Statue of Liberty. On the same floor are the Rainbow Pavilion, a spacious room for private parties, and Rainbow & Stars, an intimate cabaret and supper club. The sixty-fourth floor is a series of elegant suites and banquet rooms.

THE RAINBOW ROOM
MENU

Serves Six

Warm Quail and Foie Gras Salad

Truffled Fillet of Sole Marguery

Baked Alaska

Warm Quail and Foie Gras Salad

VINAIGRETTE

½ cup corn oil

½ cup olive oil

⅓ cup red wine vinegar

1 tablespoon minced shallot

1 to 1½ teaspoons Dijon mustard

Salt and pepper to taste

4 bunches mâche

1 small head radicchio

1 bunch frisée or chickory

1 bunch arugula

2 bunches red oakleaf lettuce

2 bunches watercress

¾ cup (1½ sticks) butter

⅓ cup corn oil

8 quail, boned

Salt and pepper to taste

9 to 12 ounces fresh uncooked foie gras*

Whisk together the vinaigrette ingredients and set aside ⅓ cup. Gently wash, dry, and mix the salad greens. Toss the mixed greens with the vinaigrette and divide the greens among 8 salad plates.

In a large sauté pan or skillet, heat 6 tablespoons of the butter and all the oil over medium-high heat until very hot. Season the insides of the quail with salt and pepper and sear the birds quickly on both sides; remove from the pan, drain on paper towels, and set aside.

continued

In another sauté pan or skillet, heat the remaining 6 tablespoons of the butter and sear the foie gras on both sides until brown. Remove the pan from the heat. Cut each quail in half lengthwise and place both halves on a plate of greens. Top with a slice of foie gras.

Return the foie gras pan to high heat and deglaze with the reserved ⅓ cup vinaigrette. Spoon the hot liquid over the foie gras and serve.

Makes 8 servings

*Available at some specialty meat shops and from D'Artagnan in Jersey City, New Jersey (mail orders are available UPS Next Day Air).

Truffled Fillet of Sole Marguery

1⅓ cups dry white wine

2 medium onions, minced

½ cup chopped fresh parsley

2 bay leaves

1 teaspoon chopped fresh thyme

2 large garlic cloves, chopped

32 large fresh mussels, scrubbed and debearded

3 cups heavy cream

4 ounces canned black truffles, minced, with juice (optional)

24 Dover sole fillets

16 large shrimp, peeled and deveined

2 tablespoons soft butter, blended with 2 tablespoons flour

½ cup chopped fresh parsley

1 cup cooked rice

In a large saucepan, place the white wine, onion, parsley, bay leaf, thyme, garlic, and mussels. Cover tightly, bring to a boil, and cook for 6 to 8 minutes, or until some of the mussels open. Remove the opened mussels with a slotted spoon, then cover the pan and cook the remaining mussels for 2 minutes longer. Remove any additional opened mussels and discard those that have not opened; reserve the poaching liquid in the saucepan. Remove the mussels from their shells, discard the shells, and set the mussels aside.

Preheat the oven to the lowest possible temperature. In another saucepan, bring the cream to a boil and cook until the volume is reduced by one half; set aside. Strain the poaching liquid through a sieve and place in a large clean saucepan. Blend in the truffles and their juice (if desired). Fold each sole fillet in overlapping thirds. Place the fillets flat in the saucepan, add the shrimp, and bring to a simmer; cover the pan and poach for 3 to 4 minutes. Transfer the sole, shrimp, and a few tablespoonfuls of the liquid to a casserole, and add the cooked mussels. Cover and place in the preheated oven to keep warm. Set 8 dinner plates in the warm oven to heat.

In a clean saucepan, cook and stir the creamed butter and flour over medium-high heat, add the poaching liquid, and reduce it to a thick syrup, being careful not to burn. Whisk in the reduced cream and continue whisking while the mixture comes to a boil. Reduce the heat and maintain the sauce at a simmer.

Mix the parsley and rice and spoon a portion into the center of each warmed plate. Surround each serving of rice with 3 sole fillets, 2 shrimp, and 4 mussels, and spoon the hot sauce over.

Makes 8 servings

Baked Alaska

SPONGE CAKE

10 eggs

1 cup sugar

½ cup (1 stick) butter, melted

1 cup sifted cake flour

½ pint chocolate ice cream

½ pint raspberry sherbet

½ pint vanilla ice cream

4 egg whites

½ cup sugar

FRUIT SAUCE

¼ cup water

¼ cup sugar

½ vanilla bean

¼ cup raspberries

¼ cup blueberries

½ cup strawberries, sliced

¼ cup brandy

To make the cake, preheat the oven to 375°. In a large bowl, beat the eggs, sugar, and butter with an electric mixer for 10 minutes. Sprinkle the flour over the egg mixture ¼ cup at a time and fold it in carefully. Pour the batter into 2 buttered and floured 9-inch round pans. Bake for 15 to 20 minutes, or until a knife inserted in the center comes out clean. Remove from the oven, set the pans on racks, and let the sponge cake cool completely. Remove the cake from the pans and cut into ¼-inch-thick slices.

On a platter, overlap slices of sponge cake to make a circle 6 or 7 inches in diameter. Pack the chocolate ice cream in a small bowl, invert, and unmold on top of the circle, and cover the ice cream with a thin layer of cake slices. Top the cake slices with a layer of raspberry sherbet, and mound the vanilla ice cream on top of the sherbet. Cover the entire dessert with a thin layer of sponge cake; freeze.

In a large bowl, beat together the egg whites until foamy, then continue to beat while adding the sugar gradually until stiff peaks form. Spoon the mixture into a pastry bag with a ½-inch tip and pipe swirls to completely cover the cake. Freeze for 2 hours.

To make the fruit sauce: In a saucepan, place the water, sugar, and vanilla bean and cook to reduce to a syrup. Remove the vanilla bean with a slotted spoon and stir in the raspberries, blueberries, and strawberries; let cool.

Just before serving, preheat the oven to 500°. Bake the dessert for 2 minutes, or until the meringue lightly browns. In a small saucepan, heat the brandy, light it with a match, and pour the flaming liquid over the baked Alaska. Serve at once, with fruit sauce.

Makes 8 to 10 servings

THE RITZ-CARLTON
BOSTON, MASSACHUSETTS

The Ritz-Carlton, Boston, has offered gracious service and the finest accommodations for over six decades and is New England's only Five-Diamond Hotel. The cherished landmark is set in the heart of Boston's Back Bay and overlooks the historic Boston Public Garden. The hotel has undergone a recent expansion and complete restoration.

Incomparable cuisine and a tradition of music have enchanted hotel guests since 1927. Rodgers and Hammerstein found inspiration at the Ritz-Carlton, writing many musical favorites there, and Tennessee Williams worked on *A Streeetcar Named Desire* during a visit. In the 1930s and 40s, more Broadway plays and musicals were created and revised at the Ritz-Carlton than any other single location in the country.

The hallowed traditions of Escoffier still reign in the Ritz-Carlton, Boston, kitchens. The elegant dining room's acclaimed menu is complemented by an extensive wine list, and piano music sets the mood for dinner and the Saturday Luncheon Fashion Show. The Grand Brunch on Sunday features chamber music. The following menu and recipes were created by chef Jean-Francis Mots.

RITZ-CARLTON, BOSTON
MENU

Serves Four

Scallop and Saffron Bisque

Salad Nanon with Truffle Dressing

Loin of Venison with Peppercorns and Lingonberries

Strawberries Romanoff

Scallop and Saffron Bisque

4 cups (1 quart) Fish Stock, page 231

2 pounds sea scallops

4 tablespoons unsalted butter

1 cup chopped onions

1½ cups chopped carrots

¼ teaspoon saffron, crumbled

4 cups (2 pints) heavy cream

Salt and freshly ground white pepper to taste

¼ cup dry white wine

2 tablespoons ½-inch-long fresh chives

In a large pot, bring the fish stock to a boil. Reduce the heat until the liquid is barely simmering. Add the scallops and poach them for 3 to 4 minutes, or until just opaque. Remove the scallops from the fish stock with a slotted spoon and immediately rinse them under cold running water; let cool. Cut the scallops into ¼-inch round slices. Set the fish stock and the scallops aside.

In a heavy saucepan, melt the butter over medium heat. Add the onions, carrots, and saffron; cover the pan and reduce the heat. Cook the vegetables for 15 minutes, stirring occasionally. Add the fish stock, heavy cream, salt, and pepper and simmer for 15 minutes, or until the vegetables are tender. In a blender or food processor, purée the soup in batches until smooth.

In a sauté pan or skillet, bring the wine to a boil over high heat; reduce the heat to medium and cook for 2 minutes to burn off the alcohol. Add the sliced scallops and toss them in the wine for 1 minute, or until just heated through. To serve, divide the scallops evenly among warmed soup bowls, pour in the bisque, and garnish with chopped chives.

Makes 6 to 8 servings

Salad Nanon

Leaves from 3 heads Boston or Bibb lettuce

6 hard-cooked eggs

½ cup walnuts, coarsely chopped

Truffle Dressing, following

6 fresh herb sprigs, such as thyme, rosemary, or sage

Wrap the washed lettuce leaves in a tea towel and refrigerate for 30 minutes to crisp. Slice the eggs into ⅛-inch slices.

Arrange the lettuce leaves on 6 chilled salad plates. Place the egg slices decoratively on the lettuce and sprinkle the salad with walnuts. Drizzle dressing over each salad and garnish with an herb sprig.

Makes 6 servings

TRUFFLE DRESSING

¼ cup balsamic vinegar

3 tablespoons red wine vinegar

¼ cup walnut oil

½ cup vegetable oil

¼ teaspoon minced garlic

1 teaspoon minced canned black truffle

2 tablespoons truffle juice (from the can or jar in which the truffle was packed)

Salt and freshly ground white pepper to taste

In a large bowl, mix all the ingredients together with a whisk.

Loin of Venison with Peppercorns and Lingonberries

1½ cups Veal Stock, page 233, or beef broth

1½ teaspoons juniper berries

1½ oranges

3 tablespoons black peppercorns

Twelve 3-ounce venison medallions*

Salt to taste

1½ tablespoons unsalted butter

¾ cup bottled lingonberries, drained

3 tablespoons 2-inch-long chives

In a saucepan, bring the veal stock or beef broth to a boil over high heat. Reduce the heat to medium, add the juniper berries, and simmer for 10 minutes. Strain the stock and set aside.

Use a zesting tool or a potato peeler to cut off wide swatches of the colored zest of the orange, leaving the white part of the rind. Cut the zest into 1-inch-long pieces and cut these into ¹⁄₁₆-inch-wide shreds. In another saucepan, blanch 2 tablespoons of the shredded orange zest in boiling water to cover for 30 seconds, then immediately rinse it under cold running water. Drain the orange zest and set it aside.

continued

Cover a work surface with waxed paper and spread the peppercorns on top of it. Rock a heavy-bottomed saucepan a few times over the peppercorns to crack them. Roll the venison in the crushed peppercorns, covering each medallion with an equal amount of pepper. Season the medallions with salt.

In a large sauté pan or skillet, melt the butter over medium-high heat. Sauté the venison for 6 minutes, turning once, and transfer the cooked medallions to a serving platter and keep warm, reserving the pan and its juices.

Add the stock to the pan. As the stock comes to a boil, scrape the pan to dissolve the browned juices. Add the orange zest and lingonberries to the stock. Reduce the sauce until it thickens slightly, just enough to lightly coat the back of a spoon. Pour the sauce over the medallions, garnish with chopped chives, and serve immediately.

Makes 6 servings

*A medallion is a round filet cut from the loin or tenderloin. A butcher dealing in high-quality meats will usually be willing to prepare them for you.

Strawberries Romanoff

¼ cup Grand Marnier

2 cups port

¼ cup plus 3 tablespoons sugar

4 pints strawberries, stemmed and halved

3 cups heavy cream

In a large bowl, combine the Grand Marnier, port, and ¼ cup of the sugar. Add the strawberries and let them macerate in the liquid for at least 2 hours in the refrigerator.

In a deep bowl, whip the cream with the remaining 3 tablespoons of sugar until it forms soft peaks. Place 1 cup of the whipped cream in a pastry bag with a star tip and refrigerate.

Just before serving, drain the strawberries and fold them into the whipped cream. Divide the strawberries and cream among 6 chilled dessert bowls. Top each portion with a decorative rosette of whipped cream.

Makes 6 servings

The Sun Valley Lodge was created as a resort for "roughing it" in luxury. In 1935, Averell Harriman, then Chairman of the Board of Union Pacific Railroad, planned to attract passenger traffic to the West by developing a destination ski resort in Ketchum, Idaho. The elegance Harriman established at the Sun Valley Lodge's inception attracted East Coast notables and Hollywood stars including Gary Cooper, Clark Gable, Ingrid Bergman, and Ernest Hemingway, who finished writing *For Whom The Bell Tolls* there.

Harriman not only put Sun Valley on the map but also revolutionized the ski industry. Sun Valley was the first full-service ski resort in the country and the first ski area anywhere in the world to use chairlifts. Today, Sun Valley has the largest vertical ski lift in North America. There is also a Nordic Center, two outdoor heated swimming pools, indoor and outdoor skating rinks, a movie theater, bowling, and stables. The Lodge encourages beginning skiers and family ski vacations. In summer there is a variety of activities to choose from, including archery, tennis, golf, hiking, swimming, hunting, riding, fishing, and soaring.

The following menu features items you might find on the Sun Valley Lodge Sunday brunch buffet. The menu and recipes were presented to *Menus and Music* by Executive Chef Claude Guigon.

Sun Valley Lodge
Menu

Serves Six

Salmon Mousse

Trail Creek Salad

Cups of Bliss

Leg of Lamb "au Barbecue"

Strawberries Dipped in White Chocolate

Salmon Mousse

COURT BOUILLON

4 cups (1 quart) water

Several sprigs parsley

A few celery leaves

1 bay leaf

1 teaspoon cracked peppercorns

A few fennel seeds or aniseeds

1 small onion, peeled and quartered

1 cup dry white wine, or ¼ cup fresh lemon juice

1 pound fillet of king salmon

3 tablespoons fresh lemon juice

½ cup mayonnaise

1 teaspoon Dijon mustard

2 tablespoons minced shallots

¼ cup minced fresh dill

In a large pot, bring all the court bouillon ingredients to a boil, simmer 20 minutes, and strain. Place the salmon fillet in a pan and carefully cover the fish with the court bouillon. Simmer over low heat, not allowing the liquid to boil, for 7 to 8 minutes. Remove the fish with a slotted spatula and drain well.

Break the fillet into flakes with a fork, place in a bowl, and combine with all the remaining ingredients. Pack into an oiled mold and chill well before serving.

Makes 4 servings

Trail Creek Salad

1 large pink grapefruit

1 large avocado

1 large peach

Crisp salad greens

DRESSING

⅓ cup vegetable oil

1 teaspoon olive oil

2 tablespoons fresh lime juice

1 teaspoon minced fresh mint

1 teaspoon brown sugar

Peel and section the grapefruit; peel and slice the avocado and peach. Place the salad greens on individual salad plates, then arrange the sliced fruits over the greens. Whisk all the dressing ingredients together and pour the dressing over the fruits.

Makes 4 servings

Cups of Bliss

12 small new potatoes (Red Bliss)

STUFFING

3 bacon slices

½ cup sour cream

2 teaspoons fresh lemon juice

4 drops Tabasco sauce

5 drops Worcestershire sauce

1 tablespoon chopped shallots

2 tablespoons chopped fresh chives

1 teaspoon minced garlic

Ground black pepper to taste

Place the unpeeled potatoes in boiling water to cover and cook until tender. Drain the potatoes and cool them in the refrigerator.

To make the stuffing, fry the bacon until crisp. Remove the bacon from the pan with a spatula and allow it to drain on paper towels. In a bowl, combine the remaining ingredients; then crumble the bacon and add it to the sour cream mixture. Blend thoroughly.

Slice the cooled potatoes in half. Cut off the bottom of each half so the cups will stand; then hollow out the potato with a melon scoop. Stuff the potato cups with the bacon and sour cream mixture.

Makes 4 servings

Leg of Lamb "au Barbecue"

One 4-pound boneless leg of lamb
1 teaspoon minced fresh mint
1 tablespoon minced fresh basil
1 teaspoon minced fresh rosemary
½ teaspoon minced fresh thyme
½ cup olive oil
Salt and pepper to taste

Cut four 1-inch-deep slits in the leg of lamb and prepare the meat for the spit. In a mixing bowl, combine the herbs, then add the oil and mix to form a paste. Season to taste. Lightly brush the lamb with the herb mixture and work it into the slits. Cook the lamb for 1½ hours on a rotisserie, or bake in a 350° oven for 2 hours for well done (180° on a meat thermometer).

Makes 4 servings

Strawberries Dipped in White Chocolate

3 ounces white chocolate
12 strawberries

Place the chocolate in a double boiler and melt over barely simmering water. Remove from heat. Dip half of each strawberry into the chocolate, shake off the excess, and set on a plastic tray or a sheet of plastic wrap. Let cool and serve.

Makes 4 servings

The Tavern on the Green is a New York City landmark located in Central Park. Originally built as a sheepfold in 1870 with rural Victorian Gothic style architecture, the building was converted to a restaurant in 1934. In 1974, Warner LeRoy began a renovation and dazzling redesign of the restaurant. He reopened it in 1976, and since then the Tavern, known for its exhuberant sense of fun, has hosted more than fifty thousand events, including parties for Broadway opening nights, movie premieres, political fundraisers, and gala anniversaries and charity events.

The Tavern on the Green is the highest-grossing restaurant in the United States, serving an average of two thousand guests per day, and it is also the most self-contained, self-supporting restaurant operation in the United States. The Tavern has its own successful gift store and its own painting, upholstery, woodworking, and printing shops. The print shop produces new menus for two meals each day, which allows the Tavern and its chef to create specials reflecting the best of what is in the market that day. The restaurant's eclectic menus are planned around the changing seasons, with dishes based on fruits, vegetables, and seafood at their peak of flavor. The Tavern on the Green's Executive Chef, Georges Masraff, created the following menu and recipes for *Menus and Music*.

Tavern On The Green Menu

Serves Twelve

*Sautéed Scallops with Mousseline of Champagne
and Pink Peppercorns*

Consommé of Lobster with Ginger and Celery

Stuffed Breast of Capon with Spinach and Mushrooms

Cinnamon Crème Brûlée

Sautéed Scallops with Mousseline of Champagne and Pink Peppercorns

36 sea scallops

Salt and pepper to taste

8 egg yolks

3 tablespoons warm water

1 tablespoon fresh lemon juice

Pinch cayenne

4 cups clarified butter, see page 231

¾ cup heavy cream, whipped

1 cup champagne

36 pink peppercorns

Heat a dry nonstick sauté pan or skillet, and sear the scallops on both sides until well colored, for a total of 3 to 5 minutes. Season with salt and pepper, set aside, and keep warm in a heatproof casserole.

In the top of a double boiler over simmering water, whisk together the egg yolks, warm water, lemon juice, and cayenne until thick and pale. Whisk in the clarified butter and blend thoroughly, then add the whipped cream, champagne, and peppercorns. Spoon the sauce onto 12 appetizer plates and place 3 scallops on top of each.

Makes 12 servings

Consommé of Lobster with Ginger and Celery

2 celery stalks

2 carrots, peeled

8 cups (2 quarts) chicken broth

1 onion, chopped

Four 1-pound live Maine lobsters

2 tomatoes, chopped

1 bay leaf

Fresh thyme and tarragon sprigs to taste

One 1-inch-long piece ginger

1 leek, finely diced

Cilantro leaves

Chop 1 celery stalk and 1 carrot and set aside. In a stockpot, bring the chicken broth to a boil and add the chopped celery, carrot, and onion. Plunge the lobsters into the boiling broth and cook for 5 minutes; remove the lobsters from the hot liquid and allow them to cool.

When cool, carefully remove the tail and claw meat and set aside (save the rest of the lobster meat for another use). Remove the heads from the lobsters. Cut the heads in half and return them to the pot. Add the tomatoes, bay leaf, thyme, and tarragon and simmer over medium-low heat for 30 minutes. Strain the consommé, allow it to cool, then cover and refrigerate for several hours, until thoroughly chilled. Skim off all the fat particles. Bring the consommé to a boil and strain through a sieve lined with cheesecloth. Set 12 shallow soup plates in a warm oven to heat.

Peel the ginger and cut it into fine julienne. In a small saucepan, blanch the ginger in boiling water to cover for 1 minute; remove the ginger with a slotted spoon. Change the water and blanch the ginger for another minute; remove. Repeat the process a third time; finely dice the blanched ginger. Finely dice the remaining carrot and celery stalk. In a medium saucepan, blanch the diced carrot, celery stalk, and leek for 1 minute in boiling water to cover; drain. Evenly divide the lobster meat, ginger, and vegetables among the soup plates and pour the hot consommé over. Garnish with cilantro leaves.

Makes 12 servings

Stuffed Breast of Capon with Spinach and Mushrooms

STUFFING

5 ounces dried morels or chanterelles

1 pound spinach, stemmed

½ cup olive oil

10 shallots, chopped

3 garlic cloves

1 pound shiitake mushrooms, chopped

1 pound white mushrooms, chopped

¼ teaspoon salt

¼ teaspoon pepper

Pinch each nutmeg, thyme, and tarragon

1 chicken breast half, skinned, boned, and coarsely chopped

4 egg whites

⅔ cup heavy cream

Dash of port

Dash of cognac

2 double capon breasts, skinned, halved, boned, and pounded flat

About 4 cups (1 quart) chicken broth for poaching (optional)

continued

SAUCE

4 cups (1 quart) chicken broth

1 onion, chopped

1 carrot, peeled and chopped

1 celery stalk, chopped

1 cup heavy cream

2 cups (4 sticks) butter, cut into pieces

Salt and pepper to taste

Rinse the dried mushrooms and soak them in hot water to cover for 10 minutes. Drain, squeeze dry, chop, and set aside. Steam the spinach for 1 minute; set aside. In a sauté pan or skillet, heat the olive oil and sauté the shallots and garlic until translucent. Add the shiitakes, white mushrooms, and dried morels or chanterelles and sauté until tender, about 2 minutes. Add the salt, pepper, thyme, nutmeg, and tarragon; remove from heat and cool.

In a blender or a food processor, purée the chicken breast and egg whites. Add the heavy cream and blend for 2 minutes. Add the port and cognac; blend. In a large bowl, combine the puréed chicken mixture and the mushroom mixture; set aside.

Place each flattened capon breast on a sheet of plastic wrap. Place spinach leaves in a single layer on top of each breast. Spoon one fourth of the stuffing evenly over each breast. Tightly roll up each breast in the plastic wrap and tie closed with a piece of white cotton string. Steam for 20 minutes, or poach in simmering chicken broth to cover for 20 minutes, if desired. (These can be cooked one day in advance.) Remove with a slotted spoon and let cool.

Meanwhile, prepare the sauce. In a large saucepan, place the chicken broth, onion, carrot, and celery. Bring to a slow boil and cook until the liquid is reduced by one fourth. Blend in the cream, whisk in the butter, and season with salt and pepper.

To serve, unwrap the stuffed capon breasts and slice them diagonally. Divide the capon slices among 12 dinner plates and top with the sauce.

Makes 12 servings

Cinnamon Crème Brûlée

8 egg yolks

⅔ cup sugar

1 vanilla bean

4 cups (1 quart) heavy cream

2 bay leaves

5 peppercorns

¼ cup milk

1 cinnamon stick

1 packed cup brown sugar

Preheat the oven to 300°. In a large mixing bowl, whisk together the egg yolks and sugar until thick and light in color; set aside.

Scrape the insides of the vanilla bean into a large saucepan. Add the cream, bay leaves, peppercorns, milk, and cinnamon stick and bring to a boil. Remove from heat and strain through a sieve. Gradually whisk the hot cream mixture into the egg yolks. Pour into twelve shallow 6-ounce ramekins. Set the cups in a baking dish and pour water into the dish to halfway up the sides of the cups. Bake in the preheated oven for 30 minutes, or until set. Refrigerate the custards for several hours, until thoroughly chilled.

Just before serving, preheat the broiler. Place 3 or 4 tablespoons of the brown sugar at a time in a small sieve and push through with the back of a spoon to evenly layer the top of each custard. Place the custards under the broiler very close to the heat until the sugar is melted and crisp, about 30 seconds to 1 minute, being careful not to burn.

Makes 12 servings

Trapp Family Lodge

The Trapp Family Lodge is a mountain sanctuary surrounded by over seventeen hundred acres in the Green Mountains of Vermont. Home of the Trapp family of *Sound of Music* fame, the Lodge is located on a hill overlooking the Stowe Valley. The general manager, Johannes von Trapp, first lived here in 1941 when the original lodge housed all the members of the famous Trapp Family Singers. That lodge burned to the ground in 1980, but was rebuilt and reopened in 1983.

In the summer guests enjoy hiking, tennis, swimming, concerts in the meadow, golf, riding, fishing, and a new fitness center. In the winter, the Lodge has over forty miles of groomed cross-country terrain, this country's first touring center, and nearby downhill skiing.

The main dining room in the Lodge presents a nightly menu featuring Austrian and French cuisine based on Vermont products whenever possible. An extensive wine list complements the meals. The following pastry dessert recipes were presented to *Menus and Music* by Marshall Faye, Pastry Chef of the Trapp Family Lodge.

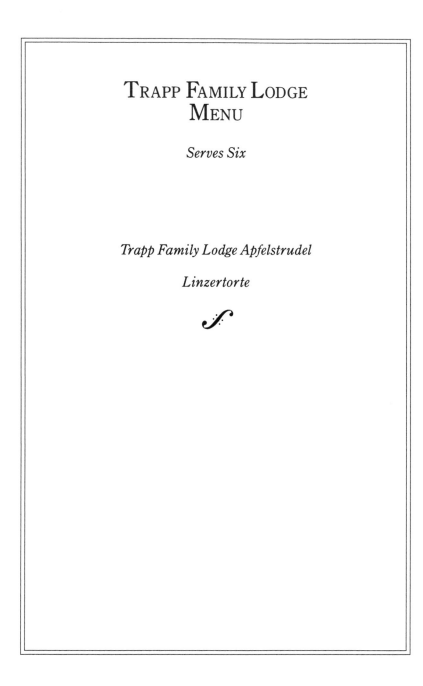

TRAPP FAMILY LODGE MENU

Serves Six

Trapp Family Lodge Apfelstrudel

Linzertorte

Trapp Family Lodge Apfelstrudel

Four 11-by-16-inch sheets fresh or thawed frozen filo dough

¾ cup (1½ sticks) butter, melted

½ cup fresh bread crumbs

2 cups sliced fresh apples

¼ cup black raisins

¼ cup golden raisins

¼ cup sugar

½ teaspoon ground cinnamon

⅛ teaspoon ground nutmeg

Pinch of ground ginger

1 egg, beaten

Powdered sugar for sprinkling

Preheat the oven to 400°. Cover a work surface with a damp cloth and lay 2 sheets of filo on top. Brush with melted butter and sprinkle with half of the bread crumbs, cover with the remaining 2 sheets of filo, and brush them with melted butter and sprinkle with the remaining bread crumbs. Arrange the apples, black and golden raisins, and almonds on top.

In a small bowl, combine the sugar, cinnamon, nutmeg, and ginger, and sprinkle this mixture on the filo. Roll up the strudel. Place in a baking pan and brush with the beaten egg and then with the remaining melted butter. Bake for in the pre-heated oven for 30 minutes, or until golden brown. Serve warm, sprinkled with powdered sugar.

Makes 6 servings

Linzertorte

1½ cups (3 sticks) butter, at room temperature

1½ cups sugar

1 egg

1½ cups walnuts, ground in a blender or nut grinder

3 cups unbleached all-purpose flour

½ teaspoon ground cinnamon

½ teaspoon ground nutmeg

¼ teaspoon ground cloves

¼ teaspoon salt

⅓ cup currant jelly

⅓ cup raspberry jam

¼ cup sliced almonds

Powdered sugar for sprinkling

Preheat the oven to 375°. In a large bowl, blend together the butter and sugar until creamy. Beat in the egg, walnuts, flour, cinnamon, nutmeg, cloves, and salt until a stiff dough is formed. Divide the dough into 4 equal parts. Grease and flour two 8-inch round cake pans. Pat 1 portion of the dough into a layer in the bottom of each pan. On a floured surface, roll the remaining 2 portions of the dough into rectangular sheets about ¼ inch thick. Cut the dough into ¾-inch-wide strips. Line the sides of each pan with 1 layer of the strips, pressing firmly.

In a small bowl, combine the currant jelly and raspberry jam, then spread half of this mixture evenly onto the bottom of each torte. Criss-cross the remaining strips of dough on top and sprinkle with sliced almonds. Bake in the preheated oven for 30 minutes or until the pastry is golden brown and the jam bubbles. Remove and let cool. Remove from the pans and sprinkle with powdered sugar.

Makes two 8-inch tortes

The Woodstock Inn & Resort is set on the village green of one of the most beautiful villages in New England. Much of Woodstock villlage has been designated a Historic District and is noted for the handsome architecture of its homes, Paul Revere bells, church spires, and covered bridge. Rockresorts's Woodstock Inn & Resort, which opened in 1969, continues a long heritage, for there has been an inn on the green since 1793. The Inn's classic New England design and appearance are combined with excellent cuisine and contemporary comfort.

The Woodstock Inn is a complete resort offering activities for every Vermont season. Guests enjoy the Robert Trent Jones golf course, tennis, horseback riding, hiking, and fishing in the spring, summer, and fall. In winter, there is family skiing, including cross-country skiing at the Ski Touring Center, and sleigh rides through the Currier and Ives landscape near the Inn. The resort's new indoor sports center offers swimming, work-outs in a state-of-the-art fitness center, tennis, and squash year round.

The following menu and recipes for a Vermont fall harvest dinner were presented to *Menus and Music* by Peter Wynia, Executive Chef of the Woodstock Inn & Resort.

WOODSTOCK INN & RESORT MENU

Serves Twelve

Acorn Squash, Apple, and Ginger Bisque

Harvest Root Salad with Sherry Vinaigrette

Maine Lobster and Cucumbers with Pasta

*Roast Loin of Veal Woodstock Inn with
Apple-Cinnamon Purée*

Bueben Spaetzle

*Indian Pudding
or
Pumpkin Brandy Charlotte Russe*

Acorn Squash, Apple, and Ginger Bisque

6 pounds acorn or butternut squash

¾ cup (1½ sticks) butter

1 pound onions, chopped

1 pound celery, chopped

1 pound carrots, peeled and chopped

2 garlic cloves, chopped

¼ cup chopped fresh ginger

1 teaspoon chopped fresh thyme

1 pound apples, peeled, cored, and chopped

1¾ cups unbleached all-purpose flour

1 cup dry white wine

16 cups (1 gallon) chicken broth

3 bay leaves

¼ cup maple syrup, or to taste

3 tablespoons brown sugar, or to taste

Salt and white pepper to taste

Cut the squash in quarters, removing the seeds and pith. Cut off the rind and cube the flesh. In a sauté pan or skillet, heat the butter and sauté the squash, onions, celery, carrots, garlic, ginger, thyme, and apples. Sprinkle with flour, whisking to form a smooth paste, and cook the mixture for 3 to 5 minutes. Stir in the white wine, then the chicken broth. Bring to a boil, then reduce heat to a simmer. Add the bay leaves, maple syrup, brown sugar, and salt and pepper. Cook for about 30 minutes, or until the vegetables are tender. Purée the soup in batches in a blender or a food processor; serve warm.

Makes 12 servings

Harvest Root Salad

SHERRY VINAIGRETTE

1 cup olive oil

2½ cups vegetable oil

¼ cup dry sherry

1 cup sherry vinegar

½ cup dry white wine

¼ cup fresh lemon juice

1 tablespoon chopped fresh chives

1 tablespoon chopped fresh thyme

1 tablespoon chopped fresh basil

Salt and pepper to taste

3 or 4 beets, peeled

2 large carrots, peeled

1¼ pounds rutabagas, peeled

14 ounces spinach, stemmed

1 large or 2 small turnips, peeled, and cut into julienne

1 celery root, peeled, and cut into julienne

6 tomatoes, peeled, seeded, and cut into julienne

To make the vinaigrette: In a bowl, mix the oils and gradually whisk in the sherry, vinegar, wine, and lemon juice. Mix in the herbs and seasonings; set aside.

Slice the beets, carrots, and rutabagus into 2-by-¼-inch strips. Blanch the vegetables separately in boiling water to cover for 5 to 10 minutes, or until al dente. If you're using the same water for all, be sure to cook the beets last.

Divide the spinach among 12 chilled plates. Arrange the vegetables on the spinach. Sprinkle with the tomatoes and spoon the sherry vinaigrette over.

Makes 12 servings

Maine Lobster and Cucumbers with Pasta

PESTO SAUCE

6 cups fresh basil leaves

¾ cup pine nuts

8 anchovies

6 small garlic cloves

1½ cups olive oil

Four 1 ¼-pound live Maine lobsters

2 tablespoons unsalted butter

2 tablespoons oil

2 cucumbers, peeled, seeded, and sliced

3 tomatoes, peeled, seeded, and diced

¼ teaspoon minced garlic

1 teaspoon minced shallot

¼ cup minced fresh dill

2 cups heavy cream

3 pounds fresh linguine or angel hair pasta

Salt and pepper to taste

Fresh parsley sprigs for garnish

To make the sauce, place the basil, pine nuts, anchovies, garlic, and olive oil in a blender or a food processor. Purée thoroughly and set aside.

Kill, cook, clean, and shell the lobsters as directed in the Method on page 78. Dice the cooked lobster meat. In a large sauté pan or skillet, heat the butter with the oil and sauté the lobster, cucumbers, tomatoes, garlic, shallot, and dill. Add the cream and pesto sauce. Boil to thicken. Set aside and keep warm.

continued

Cook the pasta in a large amount of boiling water until al dente. Drain the pasta and place on a heated platter. Pour over the pesto-cream sauce and season with salt and pepper. Garnish with parsley sprigs.

Makes 12 first-course servings, or 6 main-course servings

Roast Loin of Veal Woodstock Inn

Two 2-pound pieces boneless veal loin

¼ cup olive or other vegetable oil

Salt and pepper to taste

¼ teaspoon chopped fresh thyme

2 bay leaves, crushed

2 carrots, peeled and diced

4 celery stalks, diced

7 shallots, minced

1 garlic clove, crushed

6 tablespoons butter

1½ cups Veal Stock, page 233, or beef broth

2 cups Zinfandel

Juice of 2 lemons

1½ teaspoons cornstarch mixed with 2 tablespoons water (optional)

½ pound fresh chanterelles, chopped

2 tablespoons chopped fresh chives

Apple-Cinnamon Purée, following

Bueben Spaetzle, following

Preheat the oven to 375°. Remove any silverskin from the veal. In a sauté pan or skillet, heat the oil and sear the veal on all sides to brown lightly. Season with salt and pepper and sprinkle with thyme and bay leaves.

Place the carrots, celery, shallots, and garlic in a roasting pan. Place the veal loin on the bed of vegetables and dot with 4 tablespoons of the butter. Add ½ cup of the stock and place the pan in the preheated oven. Roast for 30 minutes, basting every 10 minutes, then add the Zinfandel, remaining stock, and half of the lemon juice. Cook the veal about 30 minutes longer, or until tender (170° on a meat thermometer).

Remove the veal from the oven and keep warm. Remove the grease from the surface of the pan juices with a large spoon. Place the baking pan on the top of the stove and stir the pan juices over heat to thicken, if necessary. (If the pan liquid is still too thin for a sauce, mix the cornstarch and water and add to the sauce.) Strain the sauce through a fine sieve, adjust the seasoning, and keep warm.

In a sauté pan or skillet, heat the remaining 2 tablespoons butter and sauté the chanterelles for 5 minutes, or until tender. Add the chives and the remaining lemon juice. Serve the veal on heated plates with the chanterelles, the apple-cinnamon purée, and the spaetzle.

Makes 12 servings

APPLE-CINNAMON PURÉE

1 pound Macintosh apples, peeled and diced

2 tablespoons butter

¼ cup fruity white wine (Northern Spy, Riesling or Chenin Blanc)

1 tablespoon sugar

¼ teaspoon vanilla extract

Ground nutmeg and cinnamon to taste

12 small pattypans (scalloped squash)

Preheat the oven to 300°. In a saucepan, combine all the ingredients except the squash and cook over low heat until the apples are tender, about 15 minutes. Meanwhile, cut the squash in half crosswise and hollow them out with a melon baller. Blanch the squash shells in boiling water to cover for 5 minutes; drain.

When the apples are tender, stir them well to blend. Purée in a blender or a food processor if you prefer a smooth sauce. Spoon the applesauce into the squash shells and heat them in the preheated oven until warmed through.

BUEBEN SPAETZLE

2 pounds potatoes, cooked and mashed

4 eggs

2¼ cups unbleached all-purpose flour

¾ cup (1½ sticks) butter, at room temperature

Salt, pepper, and nutmeg to taste

In a large bowl, combine the potatoes, eggs, flour, ¼ cup of the butter, salt, pepper, and nutmeg and blend well. Refrigerate for 2 to 3 hours, then place the chilled dough on a floured board and roll out to a sheet ½ inch thick. Cut into 1¼-inch squares; then roll up each square so that it forms a stick. Cook for 3 to 4 minutes in plenty of boiling salted water; drain. In a sauté pan or skillet, melt the remaining ½ cup butter and sauté the spaetzle for several minutes, or until golden brown.

Indian Pudding

6 cups (1½ quarts) milk

¾ cup cornmeal

1 cup raisins

3 tablespoons butter

3 eggs

¾ teaspoon ground cinnamon

¾ teaspoon ground nutmeg

¾ teaspoon ground ginger

¾ cup milk

¾ cup dark molasses

1⅓ cups brown sugar

Vanilla ice cream

Preheat the oven to 350°. Place the milk, cornmeal, raisins, and butter in a double boiler. Cook and stir over boiling water until the mixture thickens. In a large bowl, beat the eggs slightly and whisk in the spices, milk, molasses, and brown sugar. Beat the cornmeal mixture into the egg mixture.

Pour into a large buttered baking dish (cover with aluminum foil if you don't want a crust to form) and bake in the preheated oven for 45 minutes, or until set. Serve hot, with vanilla ice cream.

Makes 12 servings

Pumpkin Brandy Charlotte Russe

3 envelopes (3 tablespoons) plain gelatin

1 cup milk

1 cup canned pumpkin purée

½ teaspoon ground ginger

½ teaspoon ground cinnamon

¼ cup brandy

4¼ cups heavy cream

1 cup sugar

1 to 2 dozen ladyfingers or sponge cake strips

In the top of a double boiler, soak the gelatin in the milk for 3 minutes, then cook over boiling water until the gelatin has dissolved. Pour into a large bowl and stir in the pumpkin, ginger, cinnamon, and brandy. Let cool just to room temperature, but don't allow the mixture to thicken. In a deep bowl, whip 4 cups of the heavy cream; fold the whipped cream and sugar into the pumpkin mixture.

Line the bottom and sides of a 10-inch charlotte russe pan (any round pan 10 inches in diameter and 4 to 5 inches deep will do) with the ladyfingers or cake strips. Pour the pumpkin mixture into the pan. Place a few halved ladyfingers, baked side up, on top, and refrigerate for several hours or overnight. Invert the pan carefully onto a serving dish. Whip the remaining ¼ cup cream, garnish the charlotte russe with it, and serve.

Makes 12 servings

Basics

Clarified Butter

In a heavy saucepan, melt butter slowly over low heat. Remove from heat and let cool. Pour off the clear yellow liquid, leaving the milky residue. Store the residue in the refrigerator and use it to enrich soups and sauces. Store the clarified butter at room temperature.

Fish Stock

2 pounds fish and shellfish heads, bones, and trimmings
½ cup diced celery
2 medium onions, diced
1 cup chopped mushroom stems (optional)
2 bay leaves
¼ cup chopped fresh parsley
Thyme, oregano, salt, and pepper to taste
Water and dry white wine to cover

Wash the fish parts well. In a large saucepan, place all the ingredients and simmer for 30 minutes to 1 hour, skimming any foam from the surface. Strain through a fine-meshed sieve and adjust the seasoning.

Makes about 8 cups (2 quarts)

Pie Pastry

½ cup (1 stick) butter

1½ cups all-purpose flour

¼ teaspoon salt

3 to 4 tablespoons cold water

With a pastry cutter or 2 knives, cut the butter into the flour and salt until crumbly, or process for 10 seconds in a food procesor. Sprinkle in the water and mix with a fork, then press together in a ball (or process for 20 seconds in a food processor). Allow the dough to rest in the refrigerator for at least 30 minutes before rolling out.

Makes one 9-inch pie shell

Poultry Stock (duck, chicken, turkey, goose, or game bird)

1 onion

1 large carrot, peeled

1 celery stalk

1 leek

3 pounds poultry trimmings (heads, necks, feet, and backs)

9 parsley sprigs

5 thyme sprigs

Coarsely chop the onion, carrot, celery, and leek, and place in a stockpot. Add the poultry trimmings and herbs, and cover with water. Bring to a boil, reduce heat to a simmer, and cook uncovered for about 2 hours, skimming the surface occasionally to remove any foam. Add water as needed so that ingredients are always covered. Strain the stock through a fine sieve and reserve.

Makes about 6 cups (1½ quarts)

VEAL STOCK

2 to 3 pounds veal bones and trimmings

½ cup dry white wine

2 medium onions, coarsely chopped

2 medium carrots, peeled and coarsely chopped

2 celery stalks, coarsely chopped

¼ cup chopped fresh parsley

2 bay leaves

2 shallots, chopped

Salt and pepper to taste

Preheat the oven to 450°. In a baking dish, brown the bones and trimmings for 30 minutes, or until they are a deep brown. Deglaze the pan with the wine and transfer the bones and juices to a large saucepan. Add all the remaining ingredients and water to cover, and bring to a boil over high heat; reduce to a simmer and cook for 2 hours, skimming the surface frequently to remove any foam. Cook for an additional 1½ hours, skimming occasionally.

Strain the stock through a fine sieve and reserve. To freeze, pour the cooled stock into a plastic container and seal well; veal stock will keep for 2 months in the freezer.

Makes about 12 cups (3 quarts)

Index

S haron O'Connor is a musician and cook, and the author of the *Menus and Music* series. The cellist and founder of the San Francisco String Quartet, she has been performing with the quartet for more than ten years.

Sharon O'Connor's *Menus and Music* series combines her love of beautiful music and fine food. She is also an avid armchair traveler, who has collected festive recipes from all over America for *Holidays.* She is at work on her fourth volume, *Dinner for Two.*